Revisions

Augustinian Heritage Institute
www.augustinianheritage.org

THE WORKS OF SAINT AUGUSTINE
A Translation for the 21st Century

Part I – Books
Volume 2:

Revisions

THE WORKS OF SAINT AUGUSTINE
A Translation for the 21st Century

Revisions
(Retractationes)

including an appendix with
the *Indiculus* of Possidius

translation, notes and introduction by
Boniface Ramsey

edited by
Roland Teske, S.J.

series editor
Boniface Ramsey

New City Press
Hyde Park, New York

BR
65
.A5
E53
1990
Ser. 1
v. 2

Published in the United States by New City Press
202 Comforter Blvd., Hyde Park, NY 12538
www.newcitypress.com
©2010 Augustinian Heritage Institute

Library of Congress Cataloging-in-Publication Data:

Augustine, Saint, Bishop of Hippo.
    The works of Saint Augustine.

    "Augustinian Heritage Institute"
    Includes bibliographical references and indexes.
    Contents: — pt. 3, v .15. Expositions of the Psalms, 1-32
—pt. 3, v. 1. Sermons on the Old Testament, 1-19.
—pt. 3, v. 2. Sermons on the Old Testament, 20-50 — [et al.] — pt. 3,
v. 10 Sermons on various subjects, 341-400.
    1. Theology — Early church, ca. 30-600. I. Hill,
Edmund. II. Rotelle, John E. III. Augustinian
Heritage Institute. IV. Title.
BR65.A5E53 1990   270.2   89-28878
ISBN 1-56548-055-4 (series)
ISBN 978-1-56548-360-6 (pt. 1, v. 2)

Printed in the United States of America

For the Fischer Family
Kay and Matt and Greg and Chuck

Contents

Introduction

Augustine wrote several groundbreaking works, the most familiar of which are certainly the *Confessions*, *The Trinity* and *The City of God*. On an entirely different level stands the *Revisions*, yet it is equally groundbreaking for its being without precedent. There was no model to consult when Augustine decided "to reconsider my works from an uncompromisingly critical perspective, whether they be books or letters or sermons, and in these pages to single out for censure what I disapprove of,"[1] for no ancient author had ever done anything like it.

The *Revisions* was partially completed in 427, three years before Augustine's death—partially, because it does not include his letters and sermons, although he had begun the preliminary task of re-reading the letters[2] with the more comprehensive version of the *Revisions* in mind that he had mentioned when he described the project in his work's prologue. The two books of the *Revisions* that we possess are partial, or incomplete, in another respect as well, since they omit the few writings that Augustine produced before his decision to embrace Christianity in 386, like the lost treatise entitled *The Beautiful and the Fitting*.[3] More mysteriously, they also leave out a few of his fully Christian works, most notably *Faith in the Unseen* and *The Excellence of Widowhood*. And, it goes without saying, the seven or eight works that postdate the *Revisions* are also missing. On the other hand, however, ten works are listed that have not survived, and several letters are treated as though they were books (e.g., the two letters to Januarius) and hence are included, along with one sermon, *Faith and the Creed*, whereas other letters and sermons that could have been included are not. In some ways, then, the *Revisions* is not entirely consistent in its approach to Augustine's oeuvre.

---

1. *Revisions*, prologue 1.
2. See Letter 224,2.
3. See *Confessions* IV,13,20.

Nonetheless, it is a font of precious information. First of all, Augustine lists his writings in the chronological order in which he was aware that he had begun them. It is important to remember this when recalling that the composition of several works was spread out over many years; *Teaching Christianity*, for instance, was started in the mid-390s and not finished until the mid-420s, but, in keeping with Augustine's scheme, its place in the *Revisions* is with other works dating from the mid-390s. Many entries begin with a kind of chronological tag that is sometimes helpful in arriving at a more accurate date of composition. Frequently the circumstances in which the work was written are briefly recounted. There is usually a descriptive passage in which the work is reduced to its barest bones. When Augustine felt that he had to make changes, corrections, or observations, those followed, and in many cases they constitute the bulk of a given entry. Finally, each entry concludes with the first words of the work under discussion. Both the general plan of the *Revisions* as well as the individual arrangement of each entry, as outlined, bear testimony to a mind that was, almost uniquely among the writers of the early Church, orderly and systematic in a way that goes far toward meeting modern Western expectations.

Nearly fifteen years before he began to write the *Revisions*, Augustine pledged that, if he ever had the opportunity to go over his works as he wanted to, he would show the world that he was not biased in his own favor.[4] He honored this pledge: the *Revisions* displays frankness in acknowledging error, scrupulous concern for the full truth, a refusal to elevate the doubtful to the same level as the factual, a fear of being misleading, and a willingness to admit the fact that he did not have sufficient information to resolve some questions (most importantly, that of the origin of the soul, which he mentions as early as I,1,3 and frequently thereafter).

Some widely varied examples of this uncompromising conscientiousness, so typical of Augustine, in the *Revisions*: He often

---

4. See Letter 143,2.

worries, as he does at considerable length in I,9,3-6, that what he had said about free will at an earlier phase of his life, before the emergence of Pelagianism, might be construed as supportive of Pelagian doctrine. He regrets several times (I,26, question 62; II,18; 55,3) having suggested that the "good thief" of Lk 23:40-43 was not baptized, when in fact there is no proof that he was not. He declares in I,1,2 that he should not have used the word "omen," even jokingly, as he does in the *Answer to the Academics*, because it was not scriptural (and, by implication, had pagan resonances). He distances himself in I,7,6 from an assertion that he had borrowed from Pliny the Elder and made in *The Manichean Way of Life*, that beetles live off balls of dung; there are many people, he notes, who doubt that this is true and many who have never so much as heard of it. And in I,21,3 he says that he should not, in one of his polemical writings, have accused a Donatist bishop of deleting a phrase from a verse of scripture that did not advance his argument; he discovered some time later that the phrase was missing from a number of versions of the scriptural text and that the Donatist had not purposely left it out. Given that Donatists and Catholics were bitter enemies, and that Augustine himself was the leader of the Catholic cause, this was an especially generous admission. Such self-criticisms, of matters both major and minor, fill the pages of the *Revisions*, and, probably to the modern reader's surprise, all are treated with equal gravity.

This conscientiousness is accompanied by a certain personal reticence. Hence Augustine's description of himself in II,43,1 as "burning with zeal for the house of God" when he undertook *The City of God* is exceptional. Still more exceptional are his words at the opening of his review of the *Confessions* in II,6,1, where he indulges in a reflection that could be misconstrued as self-congratulatory: "The thirteen books of my confessions praise the just and good God for both the bad and the good that I did, and they draw a person's mind and emotions towards him. As for myself, that is how they affected me when they were being written, and that is how they affect me when they are being read. What others may think about them is up to them, but I know that they have pleased and do please many of the brothers a great deal." Elsewhere, when we might have expected a modest recognition of what the author had accomplished in a given work or an allusion to his state of mind when he was composing it, we are instead faced with the austerity of Augustine's purpose.

The *Revisions* sets before the reader's eyes in summary fashion the half-dozen or so overarching concerns that preoccupied Augustine: the bringing of neo-Platonic philosophy into the service of Catholic truth; the publicizing and even popularizing of solid scriptural exegesis, with an emphasis on the Book of Genesis and the epistles of Paul (the homilies on the Gospel of John and the First Epistle of John, along with the monumental series on all the Psalms, would have been considered had Augustine ever managed to review his sermons); and the defense of the Catholic faith in confrontation with Manicheanism, Donatism, and Pelagianism. Given that the *Revisions* was written when the battle with Pelagianism was still being fought, it makes sense that it looms the largest in Augustine's thought. And so the Pelagians are mentioned for the first time in I,7,5, in the review of a work that was written well before they appeared on the scene, while the last two entries, II,66-67, deal with problems sparked by Augustine's unyielding response to Pelagius and his disciples and to the positions that they embraced.

The reader of the *Revisions* comes away from this singular composition with the sense of having spent time with a person who was almost constantly involved in theological confrontation and whose concern for precision and truth was extraordinary.

***

Included as an appendix in this volume is the *Indiculus* (or *Indiculum* or *Elenchus*) of Possidius. Possidius, who died sometime after 437, was a close and long-time friend of Augustine and the author of his *Life*, which is the only contemporary biography of him that we possess. The *Indiculus* is a catalogue of Augustine's works that was compiled after his death in 430. It was intended to supplement the *Life*, as Possidius says in the eighteenth chapter of the biography, but in effect it also supplements the *Revisions*. Possidius, who seems to have had access to Augustine's personal library, arranged his writings according to an order of his own devising and included many of the letters and sermons that Augustine had not yet catalogued. The *Indiculus* is itself incomplete, especially in regard to the letters and sermons; it is also an occasionally eccentric work. Yet, despite these drawbacks, it is still very useful in closing several of the gaps that the *Revisions* leaves open. From the number of works that the *Indiculus* lists and that have not survived, however, we are also made regretfully aware of how much we are missing.

***

The present translation of the *Revisions* into English was made from the Latin edition in the Nuova Biblioteca Agostiniana I/II (Rome 1994), which compares the old Maurist text with the more recent text of the Corpus Christianorum; it is accompanied by an Italian translation done by Ubaldo Pizzani and preceded by an extensive and valuable introduction by Goulven Madec. Also worth consulting are the lengthy introduction, notes, and French translation, all by Gustave Bardy, in the Bibliothèque Augustinienne 12 (Paris 1950), with the Latin of the Maurist edition. There is an English translation, under the title of *The Retractations*, by Sr. M. Inez Bogan, in the series The Fathers of the Church 60 (Washington 1968); the translator follows each of Augustine's entries with some historical information about the relevant work and a short summary of it.

The translation of the *Indiculus* is based on the Latin text published by A. Wilmart in *Miscellanea Agostiniana* 2 (Rome 1931) 161-208. There is no other published English translation currently available. For an important recent study on the *Indiculus* see François Dolbeau, "La survie des oeuvres d'Augustin: Remarques sur l'*Indiculum* attribué à Possidius et sur la bibliothèque d'Ansegise," in *Augustin et la prédication en Afrique: Recherches sur divers sermons authentiques, apocryphes ou anonymes* (Paris 2005) 475-494.

Chapters[1]

---

1. There is an occasional slight discrepancy between the titles as they appear in the Chapters and as they appear in the body of the text.

Second Book

1 (28).   Two books for Simplician
2 (29).   One book in answer to the letter of Mani known as *The Foundation*
3 (30).   One book on the Christian combat
4 (31).   Four books on teaching Christianity
5 (32).   Two books against the party of Donatus
6 (33).   Thirteen books of confessions
7 (34).   Thirty-three books in answer to Faustus, a Manichean
8 (35).   Two books in answer to Felix, a Manichean
9 (36).   One book on the nature of the good
10 (37). One book in answer to Secundinus, a Manichean
11 (38). One book in answer to Hilary
12 (39). Questions on the gospels, in two books
13 (40). Notes on Job, in one book
14 (41). One book on instructing beginners in the faith
15 (42). Fifteen books on the Trinity
16 (43). Four books on the agreement among the evangelists
17 (44). Three books in answer to the letter of Parmenian
18 (45). Seven books on baptism
19 (46). One book in answer to what Centurius, one of the Donatists, presented
20 (47). Two books in answer to the questions of Januarius
21 (48). One book on the work of monks
22 (49). One book on the excellence of marriage
23 (50). One book on holy virginity
24 (51). Twelve books on the literal meaning of Genesis
25 (52). Three books in answer to the writings of Petilian
26 (53). Four books in answer to Cresconius, a grammarian of the Donatist party
27 (54). One book of proofs and testimonies in answer to the Donatists
28 (55). One book in answer to a certain Donatist
29 (56). A notice to the Donatists about the Maximianists, in one book
30 (57). One book on demonic divination
31 (58). Six questions explained in answer to the pagans
32 (59). A commentary on the Epistle of James to the twelve tribes, in one book
33 (60). Three books for Marcellinus on the punishment and remission of sins and on the baptism of infants

34 (61). One book for Constantine on the one baptism in answer to Petilian
35 (62). One book on the Maximianists in answer to the Donatists
36 (63). One book for Honoratus on the grace of the New Testament
37 (64). One book for Marcellinus on the spirit and the letter
38 (65). One book on faith and works
39 (66). A summary of the conference with the Donatists, in three books
40 (67). One book in answer to the Donatists after the conference
41 (68). One book on seeing God
42 (69). One book on nature and grace
43 (70). Twenty-two books on the city of God
44 (71). One book for Orosius in refutation of the Priscillianists and the Origenists
45 (72). Two books for the presbyter Jerome, one on the origin of the soul and another on a phrase of James
46 (73). One book for Emeritus, a bishop of the Donatists, after the conference
47 (74). One book on the deeds of Pelagius
48 (75). One book on the correction of the Donatists
49 (76). One book for Dardanus on the presence of God
50 (77). Two books for Albina, Pinianus and Melania, in answer to Pelagius and Caelestius, on the grace of Christ and original sin
51 (78). The proceedings with Emeritus, a bishop of the Donatists, after the conference, in one book
52 (79). One book in answer to a sermon of the Arians
53 (80). Two books for Count Valerius on marriage and desire
54 (81). Seven books on expressions
55 (82). Seven books of questions
56 (83). Four books on the soul and its origin
57 (84). Two books for Pollentius on adulterous marriages
58 (85). Two books in answer to an adversary of the law and the prophets
59 (86). Two books in answer to Gaudentius, a bishop of the Donatists
60 (87). One book against lying
61 (88). Four books in answer to two letters of the Pelagians
62 (89). Six books in answer to Julian
63 (90). One book for Laurence on faith, hope, and charity
64 (91). One book for Bishop Paulinus on the care to be taken of the dead

65 (92).   One book on the eight questions of Dulcitius

66 (93).   One book for Valentine and the monks with him on grace and free choice

67 (94).   One book for the aforementioned on rebuke and grace

Prologue

1. For quite a while[1] I have been reflecting on and planning on doing what I am now beginning with the Lord's help, because I do not think that it should be postponed. My task is to reconsider my works from an uncompromisingly critical perspective, whether they be books or letters or sermons, and in these pages to single out for censure what I disapprove of. No one, unless he is foolish, will dare to find fault with me because I am finding fault with my own mistakes. But if he says that I should not have said things that would afterwards be displeasing to me, he is saying what is true and agreeing with me: indeed, he is finding fault with the very same things that I am, for it would not be right for me to find fault with them if I should have said them.

2. But let everyone take what I am doing as he wishes. What was appropriate for me in this matter, though, was to apply to myself the apostolic words that say, *If we were to judge ourselves, we would not be judged by the Lord* (1 Cor 11:31).

Something else that is written, *With much speaking you will not escape sin* (Pr 10:19), terrifies me a great deal. This is not because I have written much or because much that was not written down was nonetheless put on paper when I said it (far be it from me to consider it *much speaking* when important things are being said, however numerous and copious the words may be). Rather, I fear that passage of holy scripture because from the vast number of my writings many things can doubtless be gleaned that, if not false, might at least seem or even be proven to be unnecessary. Which of his faithful did Christ not terrify when he said, *For every idle word whatsoever that a person speaks he shall give a reckoning on the day of judgment* (Mt

---

1. Since at least about the year 412, when Augustine wrote Letter 143, in which he first broached the idea of revising his works.

21

12:36)? Hence James, his apostle, also says, *Let each person be quick to listen but slow to speak* (Jas 1:19), and in another passage he says, *Let not many of you become teachers, my brothers, knowing that you are incurring a more severe judgment. For all of us cause offense in many things. If someone does not offend in word, he is a perfect man.* (Jas 3:1-2) Not even now do I claim this perfection for myself, although I am already an old man. How much less when as a young man I began to write and speak to the people! To such a degree was it my responsibility to have to speak to the people wherever I was, that I was very rarely allowed to be quiet and to listen to others and to be *quick to listen but slow to speak.*

What remains for me, then, is to judge myself under the one Teacher,[2] whose judgment of my offenses I yearn to escape. I think that there are many who become teachers when they hold different and even contradictory positions among themselves. But when all are saying the very same thing,[3] they are both saying what is true and not falling away from the teaching of the one true Teacher.[4] They do not offend when they say many things that he [i.e., the one Teacher] said but when they add their own ideas, and that in fact is how, from *much speaking*, they fall into error.

3. But I wanted to write this in order to put it into the hands of the people from whom I cannot ask back what I have already published and needs correction. I shall not even pass over what I wrote while I was still a catechumen,[5] when I

---

2. I.e., Christ; see Mt 23:8.
3. See 1 Cor 1:10.
4. Several manuscripts give a slightly different Latin text that can be translated: "But when what is said by all is the same and they are saying what is true, they are not falling away from the one true Teacher." Here the emphasis is not simply on unanimity but on unanimity in tandem with the truth. On the notion of unanimity in Christian teaching see *Baptism* III,4,6; Vincent of Lerins, *Commonitory* 2,5-6.
5. *Confessions* I,11,17 makes it clear that Augustine was a catechumen when he was a child. Two or three years before his baptism he decided to enroll once again as a catechumen, although his catechumenate at that point was of a tentative nature. See ibid. V,14,25.

continued to be involved in and puffed up with worldly literature,[6] despite having abandoned the hope that I had invested in earthly things, since even those works came to the attention of copyists and readers and are useful to read so long as some things are ignored, although, if they are not ignored, one should nonetheless not hold to their errors. Hence those who are going to read these works should not imitate me in my errors but in my progress towards the better. For whoever reads my works in the order in which they were written will perhaps discover how I have made progress over the course of my writing.[7] So that he may do so, I shall make the best possible effort to see that he is exposed to that same order.

---

6. See ibid. IX,4,7, where Augustine observes that what he wrote while at Cassiciacum testifies that he was still under the influence of "the school of pride."

7. See Letter 143,2, in which Augustine says that he is the type of person for whom writing and (spiritual and intellectual) growth go hand in hand.

First Book

1. THREE BOOKS IN ANSWER TO THE ACADEMICS
(Contra Academicos Libri Tres)[1]

1. When, therefore, I had left behind both the things that I had attained among this world's desires and those that I wanted to attain, and had brought myself to the peace of the Christian life, the first thing that I wrote, while I was still unbaptized, was the *Answer to the Academics* or *On the Academics.* My purpose was to drive from my mind with as many reasons as I could those arguments of theirs that cause many to despair of finding anything true and that prevent the wise person from assenting to anything and from accepting anything at all as clear and certain, since to them everything appears obscure and uncertain. For those arguments used to trouble me. With the Lord's mercy and assistance this was accomplished.

2. But in these same three books of mine I regret that I called upon fortune so frequently,[2] even though by this designation I did not intend some goddess or other[3] to be understood but rather the fortuitous outcome of affairs in terms of advantages or disadvantages either of the body or apart from it. And so there are words that nothing religious prohibits using—*forte, forsan, forsitan, fortasse, fortuito*[4]—although each one of them must be placed within the context of divine providence.

I was also not silent there about this when I said, "In fact, perhaps what is commonly called fortune is ruled by a kind of hidden ordering, and we call chance in things nothing else than

---

1. Written between late 386 and early 387. The Academics were adherents of the so-called New Academy, a school of thought that espoused skepticism and whose most famous representative was Cicero.
2. I,1,1; 9,25; II,1,1; 3,9; III,2,2; 3,4. See also *Revisions* I,3,2.
3. Fortuna was a Roman deity.
4. All these Latin words contain an element of chance; the first four are often translated as "perhaps," while the last can mean "by chance" or "fortuitously."

that whose reason and cause is secret."[5] I did indeed say this,
but I regret having mentioned fortune in that place, since I see
that people have the very bad habit of saying "Fortune willed it"
when they should be saying "God willed it."

In one passage I said, "It has been established in such a way
that, whether on account of our own merits or because of the
necessity of nature, the harbor of philosophy will never welcome
the divine spirit that dwells in mortal guise," and so forth.[6] Either
neither of these two things ought to have been said, because even
so the meaning would have been complete, or it would have been
enough to say "on account of our own merits," inasmuch as it is
true that our wretchedness derives from Adam, and not to add "or
because of the necessity of nature," when in fact the harsh necessity of our nature arose from the merit of a preceding wickedness.

Once again, when I said in that place, "Nothing at all—nothing that is discernable by mortal eyes, whatever any sense touches upon—is to be worshiped; all of it must be rejected,"[7] words
should have been added so that it would say "whatever any sense
of the mortal body touches upon," for there is also a sense of the
mind. But I was speaking at the time like those who say that there
is no sensing apart from the body and no sensible things except
bodily things. And so, wherever I spoke in this way, ambiguity
was not avoided, except among those who are accustomed to this
manner of speaking.

Again, I said, "What do you think it is to live happily if not to
live in accordance with what is best in man?"[8] And a little later
I explained what I meant by "what is best in man" when I said,
"Who would doubt that there is nothing else that is best in man
than the part of the soul to whose dominion whatever other parts
there are in man should submit? Should you seek another defini-

---

5. I,1,1.
6. Ibid.
7. I,1,3.
8. I,2,5.

tion, however, this part can be called mind or reason."[9] This is certainly true, for, as far as the nature of man is concerned, there is nothing in him that is better than the mind and reason. But the person who wishes to live happily must not live in accordance with that, or else he is living in accordance with man when he should be living in accordance with God,[10] so that he may be able to attain to happiness. In pursuit of that our mind should not be satisfied with itself but must submit to God.

Again, responding to one of the people with whom I was having my discussion,[11] I said, "Here you are clearly not in error, which I would gladly wish might be an omen for you in what follows."[12] Although this was said not seriously but lightly, still I wish that I had not used that word. Indeed, I do not remember having read "omen" either in our sacred scriptures or in the writings of any ecclesiastical author at all, despite the fact that "abomination," which is frequently found in the divine books, derives from it.[13]

3. In the second book, that near-fable about *philocalia* and *philosophia*—that "they are sisters and begotten of the same parent"[14]—is utterly inept and foolish.[15] For either what is called *philocalia* only has to do with trifles and for that reason is in no way related to *philosophia*; or, if this word is honorable because in Latin it means the love of beauty (and it is the true and loftiest beauty of wisdom), then *philocalia* is the very same thing as

9. Ibid.
10. See 1 Pt 4:6.
11. The people involved in this discussion were the friends who had accompanied Augustine to Cassiciacum, as well as Monica and his son Adeodatus.
12. I,4,11.
13. Augustine's rejection of the word "omen" is undoubtedly based on its connection with pagan superstition. He correctly derives abomination from omen, but he is incorrect in saying that omen is not to be found in the Bible, since in at least one Latin translation of scripture with which he might have been familiar it appears in 1 K 20:33. See the note in Migne, PL 32,586. In any event omen is a Latin word, and Augustine's information comes from consulting a Latin translation rather than the Bible's original Hebrew or Greek.
14. II,3,7.
15. The two words are Greek and mean, respectively, "love of beauty" (as Augustine explains a few lines later) and "love of wisdom."

philosophia when it comes to incorporeal and lofty matters and they are in no respect like two sisters.

In another passage, when I was discussing the soul, I said "to return more safely to heaven."[16] But I would have spoken more safely had I said "to go" rather than "to return," because of those who think that human souls have been thrust into these bodies on account of the merits of their sins after having fallen from or been cast out of heaven.[17] But I myself did not have any doubts about saying this because I said "to heaven" as if I were saying "to God," who is its maker and creator. As the blessed Cyprian did not hesitate to say, "For, since we possess a body from the earth and a spirit from heaven, we ourselves are earth and heaven,"[18] and as it is written in the Book of Ecclesiastes, *The spirit returns to God who gave it* (Eccl 12:7). Of course this is to be understood in such a way as not to run afoul of the Apostle, who says, *Not having yet been born, they did nothing good or evil* (Rom 9:11). There is no question, then, that God himself is, as it were, the original place of the soul's happiness. He did not, to be sure, beget it from himself, but he did not create it from some other thing, as he created the body from the earth. Regarding its origin, how it comes to be in a body, whether it is from that single person who was created first, when the man was made into a living soul,[19] or whether individual ones similarly come into being for individual persons, I did not know then and I still do not know.[20]

---

16. II,9,22.
17. This idea is found in several pagan writers and, among Christians, most notably in Origen; see Henri Crouzel, *Origen*, trans. by A. S. Worrall (San Francisco 1989) 205-218.
18. See Cyprian, *The Lord's Prayer* 16. Cyprian was the bishop of Carthage and died a martyr in 258. He was the author of several influential works, most notably *The Unity of the Catholic Church*. In Augustine's time he seems to have been considered the great hero of North African Christianity and its most authoritative representative, and Augustine regularly called on him to refute Donatism; despite the fact that his theology was sympathetic to what would later be qualified as Donatist tendencies, he never lapsed into schism, as the Donatists did. Augustine refers to him not only here but in two other passages in the *Revisons*—II,1,1; 18 (where he is given glowing praise).
19. See Gn 2:7.
20. This subject is discussed at length in *The Soul and its Origin*. See *Revisions* II, 56. It also appears in *Revisions* II,45.

4. In the third book I said, "If you are looking for my opinion, I think that man's highest good is in the mind."[21] It would have been more correct if I had said "in God," for it is he himself, as its highest good, that the mind enjoys so that it may be happy.

And I also regret that I said, "One may clearly swear by everything divine."[22]

Again, what I said about the Academics—that they knew the true, calling the likeness of it a likeness of the true, and that very likeness of the true, which they assented to, I called false[23]—was not said correctly for two reasons: either because that would be false which was in some way similar to something true, for in its own class even that is true, or because they assented to those false things, which they said were like the true, although they assented to nothing and insisted that a wise person assented to nothing. But it happened that I spoke this way about them because they also referred to this very likeness of the true as probable.

Likewise, the praise with which I so greatly extolled Plato and the Platonists (or the Academic philosophers)[24] was most inappropriate for these impious persons and has rightly displeased me; it is especially in the face of their great errors that Christian teaching must be defended.

There is also the fact that, in comparison with the arguments of Cicero which he made in his *Academica*, I said that mine were trifles.[25] It was by them that I refuted his arguments with the most unassailable reasoning. Although this was said in a humorous vein and would seem rather like irony, nonetheless it ought not to have been said.

This work begins in this way: "If only, Romanianus, . .a man suited for herself."

21. III,12,27.
22. III,16,35.
23. III,18,40.
24. II,10,24; III,17,37; 18,41. Plato is in fact considered the founder of what came to be known as the Old Academy; the philosophical link between the Old and the New is somewhat tenuous.
25. III,20,45. The *Academica* was Augustine's primary source for the teachings of the New Academy.

2. ONE BOOK ON THE HAPPY LIFE
(De Beata Vita Liber Unus) [26]

It happened that I wrote a book on the happy life not after the books on the Academics but while I was occupied with them. It was begun on the occasion of my birthday and was completed after three days of discussion, as it itself quite clearly indicates. In this book we who were searching together[27] agreed that there was no happy life apart from the perfect knowledge of God. I regret, however, that in it I made more of Manlius Theodorus, to whom I dedicated the book, than I ought to have, although he was a learned and Christian man;[28] that I also often referred to fortune in it;[29] and that I said that the happy life resided only in the soul of a wise person during the time of this life, in whatever state his body might be,[30] although the Apostle hopes for the perfect knowledge of God—meaning that than which none greater can exist for a person—in the life to come,[31] which alone can be called the happy life, when the incorruptible and immortal body[32] will be subordinate to its spirit without any disturbance or reluctance.

As a matter of fact I found this book with an omission in our codex and lacking no small amount, and that is how it was transcribed by some of the brothers; even to this day I have not found a complete copy of it with which I could make corrections when writing these revisions.

This book begins in this way: "If to the harbor of philosophy."

---

26. Written on November 13, 386 and over the course of several days thereafter. November 13th was Augustine's birthday.
27. I.e., the group of persons who were with Augustine at Cassiciacum.
28. 1,5. Manlius Theodorus was an important personage in Milan and was named a consul in 398; he exercised a beneficial influence on Augustine.
29. Ibid. See *Revisions* I, 1,2.
30. 4,25
31. See 1 Cor 13:12.
32. See 1 Cor 15:53.

3. Two Books On Order
(De Ordine Libri Duo)[33]

1. During the same period, while the books on the Academics were being written, I wrote two other books on order, in which the great question is explored as to whether the ordering of divine providence includes all things good and evil. But when I realized that this was something difficult to understand and that it was almost impossible to make the matter comprehensible to the people with whom I was discussing it,[34] I decided to talk instead about the order of studies whereby one can proceed from corporeal to incorporeal realities.

2. But I regret that in these books as well the word "fortune" often appears;[35] that I did not add the words "of the body" when I mentioned the senses of the body;[36] that I attributed a great deal to the liberal disciplines, which many holy persons know very little about (while several of those who do know something about them are not holy);[37] that I referred to the Muses as some sort of deities, albeit jokingly;[38] that I called astonishment a vice;[39] that I said that philosophers who were not endowed with true piety shone with the light of virtue;[40] and that—not in the person of Plato or the Platonists[41] but on my own—I spoke of two worlds, one sensible and the other intelligible, as though the Lord had wanted to signify such a thing because he did not say, "My kingdom is not of the world," but rather, *My kingdom is not of this world* (Jn 18:36),[42] although it could also be found to have been said in some other manner of speaking. If, to be sure, some other world was being

---

33. Written between late 386 and early 387.
34. I.e., those who had accompanied Augustine to Cassiciacum.
35. II,9,27. See *Revisions* I,1,2.
36. I,1,3. See *Revisions* I,4,2.
37. I,5,15; 8,24; II,14,39. Augustine's unease with the liberal disciplines, so closely connected with pagan culture, is apparent in, e.g., *Confessions* I,12,19-18,31; *Teaching Christianity* II,39,58-42,63.
38. I,3,6; 8,24; II,14,39.
39. I,3,8.
40. I,11,31.
41. See Plato, *Republic* 508c.
42. I,11,32.

signified by the Lord Christ, it could more easily have been understood in the passage where [it is said that] there will be *a new heaven and a new earth* (Rv 21:1), when what we pray for when we say *thy kingdom come* (Mt 6:10) will be achieved. Indeed, Plato was not mistaken when he spoke of an intelligible world, if we are willing to focus not on this expression, which is not current in ecclesiastical language, but on the reality itself. In fact what he called the intelligible world was the very eternal and immutable reason by which God made the world. If someone denies that this exists, he is necessarily saying that God made irrationally what he made or that, when he was making it or before he made it, he did not know what he was making if he had within himself no reason to make it. But if, as was the case, he did, Plato seems to have called this very same thing the intelligible world. Nonetheless we ourselves would not have used this expression if at the time we had been sufficiently educated in ecclesiastical literature.

3. I also regret that when I said, "The greatest effort must be given to the best conduct," I added soon after, "For our God will be unable to hear us otherwise, but he will most easily hear those who live well."[43] For this was said as though God would not hear sinners, which someone said in the gospel;[44] but that was one who did not yet know Christ, by whom he had already been enlightened in his body.

I also regret that I bestowed so much praise on the philosopher Pythagoras,[45] so that the person who hears or reads it could think that I believed that there were no errors in Pythagorean doctrine, although there are many, and they are major ones.

This work begins in this way: "The ordering of things, Zenobius."

---

43. II,20,52.
44. See Jn 9:31.
45. II,20,53-54. Pythagoras, whose doctrine Augustine refers to in *Order* as "venerable and nearly divine," was a Greek philosopher and religious reformer active in southern Italy about 530 B.C. His numerology was especially influential in antiquity and figured importantly in Augustine's thought.

4. Two Books Of Soliloquies
(Soliloquiorum Libri Duo)[46]

1. Meanwhile I also wrote two volumes in keeping with my zeal for and love of searching out the truth, through reason, in regard to matters that I especially desired to know. I questioned myself and responded to myself as though we were two persons, reason and I, despite the fact that I was alone, and that is why I entitled this work *Soliloquies*. But it remained incomplete, yet such that in the first book the question was raised and more or less answered as to what a person ought to be like who desires to acquire wisdom, which is of course acquired not by bodily sensing but through the mind, and at the end of the book a conclusion is reached, by a sort of reasoning process, that those things that truly exist are immortal. In the second book, however, the issue of the immortality of the soul is debated for a long time and not resolved.

2. In these books I do not approve of what I said in a prayer: "O God, who have not wished any but the pure to know what is true."[47] For the response can be made that even many of those who are not pure know many true things. Nor is it defined in this passage what is meant by the true, which only the pure can know, and what it means to know.

There is also this which was said there: "O God, whose kingdom is the whole world, *quem*[48] the senses do not know."[49] If God is intended here, words should have been added so that it would say "whom the senses of the mortal body do not know." If, however, it was the world that was spoken of which the senses do not know, that one is correctly understood which is to come by means of a new heaven and a new earth,[50] but even in that case

---

46. Written between late 386 and early 387.
47. I,1,2.
48. The Latin masculine relative pronoun *quem* may in this context mean either "whom" or "which"; the former would refer to God, the latter to the world. Augustine does not seem to remember which of the two he intended to refer to. Augustine elsewhere confesses forgetfulness as to what he once meant. See *Revisions* I,5,3.
49. I,1,3.
50. See Is 65:17;66:22; 2 Pt 3:13; Rv 21:1.

those words should have been added which would say "the senses of the mortal body." But I was still speaking then according to the custom whereby sensing is properly referred to the body, and what I have already noted above in that regard did not need to be constantly repeated; nonetheless this should be recalled wherever this expression is to be found in my writings.[51]

3. And when I said of the Father and the Son, "He who begets and he whom he begets is one,"[52] it should have been said "are one," as Truth himself clearly says when he states, *I and the Father are one* (Jn 10:30).[53]

And I also regret that I said that "in this life the soul is happy when it has known God,"[54] which is not the case except perhaps in hope.

Again, what I said, "There is not one way to a union with wisdom,"[55] does not sound right. It is as though there were another way apart from Christ, who said, *I am the way* (Jn 14:6). This offense to pious ears should have been avoided, then, although that universal way is one thing, while the ways that we speak of in the Psalms—*Lord, make known to me your ways, and teach me your paths* (Ps 24:4)—are another.

And what I said there, "These sensible things should be utterly fled from,"[56] should be treated with caution, lest we be thought to agree with the opinion of the false philosopher Porphyry, when he said that every body ought to be fled from.[57] I myself did not say "all things" but rather "these things"—namely, corruptible things. But this ought rather to have been said. Such sensible things will

---

51. See *Revisions* I,3,2.
52. I,1,4.
53. Augustine passes over the fact that this correction not only is scripturally based but also represents a grammatical improvement.
54. I,7,14.
55. I,13,23.
56. I,14,24.
57. See Porphyry, *Ad Marcellam* 8.32.34. This opinion is also cited, and repudiated, in *The City of God* X,29; XII,27; XIII,17; XXII,26. The Greek philosopher Porphyry (c. 234-c.301), who studied under Plotinus, was both a sharp critic of Christianity and, with Plotinus, a significant influence on Augustine's thought. Augustine usually refers appreciatively to Porphyry, and his words here are exceptional.

not, however, exist in the *new heaven and the new earth* (Is 65:17; 66:22; 2 Pt 3:13; Rv 21:1) of the world to come.

4. Again, in a certain passage I said that "through study those who are schooled in the liberal disciplines undoubtedly draw out those things that had been covered over through forgetfulness and in a certain way dig them up again."[58] This too I reject. For it is more believable that even those who are not proficient in them give true answers with regard to certain disciplines when they are asked in the right way, because the light of eternal reason is present to them (to the degree that they can grasp it) when they have a glimpse of these unchangeable truths, not because they knew them at one time and forgot them, which was the view of Plato and others like him.[59] I argued against their opinion, as the occasion presented itself in the work that I had undertaken, in the twelfth book of *The Trinity*.[60]

This work begins in this way: "Considering many different things within myself."

5. One Book On The Immortality Of The Soul
(De Immortalitate Animae Liber Unus)[61]

1. After the books of the *Soliloquies*, and when I had already returned to Milan from the country, I wrote a book on the immortality of the soul that I had wanted to be a kind of reminder to myself to finish the *Soliloquies*, which had remained unfinished. But somehow, unbeknownst to me, it fell into people's hands and is mentioned among my shorter works. It is, first of all, so obscure on account of its complicated reasoning and its brevity that, when I read it, it taxes even my own attention and I myself can barely understand it.

2. Considering nothing else than the souls of men, I said in a certain argument in the same book, "There cannot be a discipline[62]

---

58. II,20,35.
59. See Plato, *Phaedo* 72e; *Meno* 81e-86b.
60. See *The Trinity* XII,15,24.
61. Written at the beginning of 387.
62. The Latin *disciplina*, which is used in these lines, means a learned or acquired knowledge, while *scientia*, which translates "knowledge," suggests knowledge in its broadest connotation.

in that which learns nothing."[63] And again, in another passage I said, "Knowledge does not embrace anything unless it pertains to some discipline."[64] I was not thinking that God does not learn a discipline; rather, he possesses the knowledge of all things, in which there is also the foreknowledge of future things. The same sort of thing was brought up elsewhere: "Nothing has life with reason but the soul,"[65] for God's life is not without reason, since with him there is both the highest life and the highest reason.

And there is what I said a little before that: "That which is understood is always the same,"[66] although the mind, which is certainly not always the same, is also understood.

But what I said, "The soul cannot be separated from eternal reason, because it is not joined to it spatially,"[67] I would certainly never have said if at the time I had been sufficiently educated in the sacred writings to have recalled what is written: *Your sins are causing a separation between yourselves and God* (Is 59:2). From this we are made to understand that separation can be spoken of even with regard to those things that have been joined not in terms of place but incorporeally.

3. I have been unable to remember what I meant when I said, "A soul does not exist in this world if it lacks a body."[68] For do not the souls of the dead lack a body, or do they not exist in this world, as though the nether regions were not in this world?[69] But because I understood the lack of a body in a good sense, perhaps I was referring to bodily evils by the term "body." But if that is the case, I used the word in an extremely unusual way.

---

63. 1,1.
64. Ibid.
65. 4,5.
66. 1,1.
67. 6,11.
68. 13,22. On Augustine's forgetfulness see p. 33, n. 48.
69. In the common understanding of the early Church, the nether regions (*inferi* in Latin) were simply the place where the souls of the dead, both good and bad, waited until the Final Judgment; they were located beneath the surface of the earth and are not to be confused with the place of torment, although they are sometimes referred to as hell. See also *Revisions* II,24,2.

This too was said rashly: "From the highest essence a form is bestowed upon the body through the soul, whereby it exists to the extent that it exists. It is through the soul, then, that the body exists, and it is for this very reason that it is animated, whether universally, as in the case of the world, or particularly, as in the case of each ensouled creature in the world."[70] All of this was said very rashly. This book begins in this way: "If a discipline exists anywhere."

6. ONE BOOK OF THE BOOKS ON THE DISCIPLINES
(De Libris Disciplinarum Liber Unus)[71]

At the same time, when I was about to be baptized at Milan, I also attempted to write books on the disciplines. I was questioning those who were with me and who were not repelled by studies of this sort; I wanted to lead them to and to arrive myself at incorporeal things by way of corporeal ones, and to do so as though by sure steps. But I was only able to complete one book, *Grammar*,[72] on those disciplines, which afterwards disappeared from my safekeeping, and six books on music,[73] which only go as far as the part that is referred to as rhythm. But I wrote those same six books after having been baptized[74] and after having returned to Africa from Italy, since I had barely started on that discipline while I was in Milan. Of the other five disciplines that I started on there—dialectic,[75] rhetoric, geometry, arithmetic, philosophy—only the beginnings survived, and we lost them too, but I think that they are in the possession of others.

---

70. 15,24.
71. The disciplines mentioned here can otherwise be referred to as the liberal arts; Augustine lists the customary seven in the body of this entry.

    From this point the numbering of the chapters differs from that used in the critical edition of the Corpus Scriptorum Ecclesiasticorum Latinorum (CSEL). The latter numbering appears in parentheses.
72. Written in early 387 and no longer extant, although there is a possibility that at least one abridgement exists.
73. See *Revisions* I,11.
74. I.e., after Easter 387.
75. A brief, incomplete and anonymous work entitled *On Dialectic* has survived from this period; although its authorship is disputed, most modern scholars would agree that it is by Augustine.

7 (6). Two Books On The Catholic Way Of Life And The Manichean Way Of Life
(De Moribus Ecclesiae Catholicae Et De Moribus Manichaeorum Libri Duo)[76]

1. When I was at Rome after having been baptized and was unable to bear in silence the boasting of the Manicheans about their false and fallacious continence, or abstinence, by means of which, in order to deceive the ignorant, they put themselves above true Christians (with whom they really cannot be compared), I wrote two books; one of them was *The Catholic Way of Life* and the other was *The Manichean Way of Life*.

2. In *The Catholic Way of Life*, then, when I provided a proof text in the passage that reads, *On account of you we are being afflicted the whole day; we have been treated like sheep for the slaughter* (Ps 43:22; Rom 8:36),[77] the faultiness of our codex misled me, as one less mindful of the scriptures, since I was not yet familiar with them.[78] For other codexes of the same translation do not have *on account of you we are being afflicted* but *on account of you we are being afflicted with death*, which others have expressed with the single phrase, *we are being put to death*.[79] The Greek books indicate that this is more correct. It was from that language, hewing closely to the seventy translators of the ancient divine scriptures,[80] that a translation was made into Latin. And yet I have discussed many things while using that phrase—that is, *on account of you we are being afflicted*—and as far as those matters

---

76. Written between the end of 387 and the beginning of 388. This is the first of several works directed against the Manicheans, a religion that dated to the second half of the third century and that had a number of aspects in common with orthodox Christianity. Its most noteworthy doctrine distinguished the God of the Old Testament from that of the New and posited an evil principle co-eternal with the good God. Augustine himself had been drawn to Manicheanism before his conversion.
77. I,9,14.
78. Augustine seems not to have devoted himself to a serious study of the Bible until 391, when he was ordained a presbyter. See Letter 21,3-6.
79. The Latin says, "with one word, *mortificamur*."
80. Augustine is referring to the Septuagint, a Greek translation of the Old Testament made, according to Jewish legend, by seventy-two (not seventy) Jewish elders in third-century B.C. Alexandria.

themselves are concerned I do not disapprove of them as false. But from these particular words, I did not show the harmony of the Old and New Testaments that I wanted to show. That is why I said that error crept up on me; from other proof texts, however, I have adequately indicated that very harmony.

3. Likewise, a little later I provided a proof text from the Book of Wisdom from our codex, in which this was written: *For wisdom teaches sobriety and justice and virtue* (Wis 8:7).[81] And while using these words I did indeed say some things that were true, but discovered from a faulty text. For what is truer than that wisdom teaches the truth of contemplation, which I thought was signified by the term sobriety, and uprightness of action, which I wished to be understood by the two others, justice and virtue, although more accurate codexes of the same translation have *For it teaches sobriety and wisdom and justice and virtue*? By these terms the Latin translator named those four virtues that are very frequently mentioned by philosophers.[82] He called temperance sobriety; he applied the word wisdom to prudence; he called fortitude by the term virtue; and he translated justice alone by its own name. Long after that we found these four virtues in the same Book of Wisdom, called by their own names, just as they are called by the Greeks.

Again, what I put down from the book of Solomon, *Vanity of the vain, said Ecclesiastes* (Eccl 1:2),[83] I read in quite a number of codexes, but that is not what the Greek has. It has *vanity of vanities*, which I saw afterwards, and I found that those Latin ones that have *vanities* and not *the vain* are more correct.[84] Nonetheless, whatever I said based on this faulty text appears to be true, as the facts themselves bear out.

---

81. I,16,27.
82. See, e.g., Plato, *Laws* I,631; *Republic* IV,428ff; Cicero, *De finibus* II,51; *De officiis* I.
83. I,21,39.
84. The Latin for *vanity of the vain* and *vanity of vanities* is, respectively, *vanitas vanitantium* and *vanitas vanitatum*. *Vanitantium* seems to be a Latin biblical neologism; it occurs frequently in Augustine—e.g., in *The Magnitude of the Soul* 33,76; *True Religion* 21,41; 33,61; *Confessions* VIII,11,26; *The City of God* XX,3.

4. But what I said, "The very one whom we wish to know"—
that is, God—"we must first love with a complete charity,"[85]
would have been better said by using "sincere" rather than
"complete," lest perhaps it be thought that our charity for God
will not be greater when we shall see *face to face* (1 Cor 13:12).
That, indeed, is how it should be taken, as though "complete"
is being said in terms of that which cannot be greater as long
as we are walking by faith,[86] for it *will* be complete—no! most
complete[87]—but by vision.

Again, what I said about those who assist the needy—that
"they are called merciful, even if they are wise to the extent that
they are disturbed by no anguish of soul"[88]—ought not to be
taken as though I had said that there are such wise people in this
life, for I did not say "since they are," but I said "even if they are."

5. In another passage I said, "But when this human love has
nourished and strengthened the soul that cleaves to your breast,
and it has become capable of following God, when his majesty
has begun to open itself as much as suffices for a person while he
is dwelling on this earth, such ardor of charity is born in him and
such a blaze of divine love rises up in him that, when all his vices
have been burned away and the person is sanctified and purified,
it is sufficiently clear how divinely it was said, *I am a consuming
fire* (Heb 12:29)."[89] The Pelagians could think that I said that this
perfection could be acquired in this mortal life.[90] But they should
not think this. The ardor of charity, once it has become capable
of following God and is great enough to consume all vices, can
indeed be born and increase in this life. Yet that does not mean
that, because it is born, it can be perfect, such that no vice dwells
in a person, although that thing which is so great is perfected by

---

85. I,25,47.
86. See 2 Cor 5:7.
87. Reading *plenissima* rather than *plenissimus*.
88. I,27,53.
89. I,30,64.
90. The Pelagians were exponents of the position that spiritual perfection was within
    human capabilities.

the same ardor of charity (where it can be perfected and when it can be perfected), and like the bath of regeneration[91] it purges away the guilt of all the sins that human birth has brought upon itself and human wickedness has contracted, so that that perfection purges away the stain of all the vices without which human weakness cannot exist in this world. That is also how what the Apostle says is to be understood: *Christ loved the Church, and he gave himself for her, cleansing her by a bath of water in the word, so that he might show to himself a glorious Church that has no spot or wrinkle or anything of the sort* (Eph 5:25.27). For here [i.e., on earth] is the *bath of water in the word* by which the Church is cleansed. But since the whole Church says as long as it is here, *Forgive us our debts* (Mt 6:12), it is certainly not here *without spot or wrinkle or anything of the sort*. But, from what she accepts here, she is brought to that glory and perfection which does not exist here.[92]

6. In the other book entitled *The Manichean Way of Life* I said, "The goodness of God arranges all those things that fall away in such a way that they exist where they can most appropriately exist, until through ordered movements they return to that from which they fell away." That all things "return to that from which they fell away" must not be understood in the way that Origen understood it.[93] It applies only to the things that return. For those who are punished by an eternal fire do not return to the God from whom they fell away, although all things that fall away are arranged in such a way that they exist where they can most appropriately exist, because even those who do not return exist most appropriately in punishment.

In another passage I said, "Almost no one doubts that beetles live off dung rolled up in a ball and buried by them."[94] There are

---

91. See Tit 3:5.
92. Augustine is concerned elsewhere as well that Eph 5:27 will be misunderstood as applying to the Church in this world rather than to the eschatological Church. See *Revisions* I,19,9; II,18.
93. See Crouzel 205-218.
94. II,17,63. See Pliny the Elder, *Natural History* IX,34,98.

many, though, who doubt whether this is true, and there are many who have never even heard of it.

This work begins in this way: "In other books I think that we sufficiently treated."

8 (7). ONE BOOK ON THE MAGNITUDE OF THE SOUL
(De Animae Quantitate Liber Unus)[95]

1. In the same city [i.e., Rome] I wrote a dialogue in which many questions are raised and discussed about the soul—namely, where it comes from, what sort of thing it is, how big it is, why it has been given to a body, what sort of thing it becomes when it comes to a body, and what sort of thing when it leaves.[96] But because its magnitude was discussed very carefully and in very great detail, with the result that we showed, as much as we could, that it had no bodily magnitude and was still something great, the entire book took its title from this one investigation, so that it is called *The Magnitude of the Soul*.

2. In this book I said, "It seems to me that the soul has brought with itself all the arts, and that what is called learning is nothing else than remembering and recalling."[97] This ought not to be taken as though it were being affirmed that the soul at some time lived either here in another body or elsewhere, whether in the body or apart from the body, and that what a person responds to when questioned he learned previously in another life because he did not learn it here.[98] For it is possible, as we have already said before in this work,[99] that this could be the case because it is an intelligible nature and is also linked not only to intelligible things but even to immutable ones and, because it [i.e., the soul] has been ordered in such a way that, when it directs itself to those things to which it is linked or to its very self, it responds truth-

---

95. Written in 388.
96. 1,1.
97. 20,34.
98. The idea is Platonic. See also *Revisions* I,4,4 and p. 35, n. 59.
99. See *Revisions* I,4,4.

fully to them to the degree that it sees them. It has not of course brought all the arts with itself in that way, nor does it possess them within itself, for it can say nothing of the arts that pertain to the senses of the body—as is the case with much of medicine and all of astrology—apart from what it learns here. But there are things that the intelligence alone grasps, by reason of what I have said here, and, when it has been adequately questioned either by itself or by another, it responds with what it remembers.

3. In another passage I said, "While I am, so to speak, giving precepts to you, I would like to say more here and to restrict myself to doing nothing else than rendering an account to myself, to whom I owe it the most."[100] I think that there I ought to have said "rendering an account to God, to whom I owe it the most." But a person must first render an account to himself so that, when he has taken a step at that point, as it were, he may rise up from there and be brought to God, like that younger son who first turned back to himself and then said, *I shall arise and go to my father* (Lk 15:18). That was why I spoke that way. Shortly after that I added, "And thus a slave becomes his master's friend."[101] Hence, when I said, "myself, to whom I owe it the most," I referred to human beings, for I owe this more to myself than to other human beings, but to God more than to myself.

This book begins in this way: "Because I see that you have a great deal of leisure."

9 (8). THREE BOOKS ON FREE CHOICE
(De Libero Arbitrio Libri Tres)[102]

1. When we were still living at Rome, we wanted to discuss and examine where evil comes from. And this we discussed in such a way that a considered and extended process of reasoning,

---

100. 28,55.
101. Ibid. The idea is taken from Horace, *Satirae* II,7,2-3.
102. Begun in 388 and completed between 391 and 395. In 391 Augustine was ordained a presbyter in Hippo, and in 395 he became a bishop.

in keeping with our capacities and through discussion and with God's help, would bring to our understanding, as much as we were capable of, what we who were subject to divine authority already believed about this matter. And because, after a careful and reasonable discussion, we agreed that evil arises from nothing but the free choice of the will, that same discussion produced three books that were called *Free Choice*. I completed the second and third of these in Africa, when I was already ordained a presbyter in Hippo Regius, as I was able to do so at that time.

2. In these books so many things were discussed that a number of incidental questions, which I was unable to resolve or which at the time required a lengthy conversation, were postponed. The result was that—whether from both sides or rather from all sides of these same questions, when it was unclear which side had a better claim upon the truth—our process of reasoning brought us to the conclusion that, whichever of the answers might be true, God would be believed or would even be shown to be praiseworthy.

This discussion was initiated on account of those who deny that the origin of evil proceeds from the free choice of the will and who contend, if that is the case, that God, the creator of all natures, is to be blamed. In the same way, in keeping with the error of their impiousness (for they are Manicheans), they want to introduce a kind of immutable nature of evil that is coeternal with God.[103] But, because of the question that was before us, there is no discussion in these books about the grace of God, whereby he has predestined his chosen ones in such a way that he himself prepares the wills of those among them who already exercise free choice. When, however, an occasion presented itself for mentioning this grace, it was mentioned in passing but not defended with careful reasoning, as though it were the object of the discussion. For it is one thing to examine where evil comes from and another to examine how to return to one's original condition or to attain to a higher good.

103. See note p. 38, n. 76.

3. Hence, the recent heretics, the Pelagians,[104] who insist upon the free choice of will to such a degree that they leave no place for God's grace, since they insist that it is bestowed according to our merits, should not boast as though I had taken up their cause, because I said many things in these books on behalf of free choice, which the purpose of that discussion required.[105]

Indeed, in the first book I said, "Crimes are punished by God's justice," and I added, "for they would not be justly punished unless they were committed by the will."[106]

Again, when I was showing that a good will itself was such a great good that it is rightly preferred to all bodily and external goods, I said, "You see now, therefore, as far as I can tell, that it has to do with our will that we either enjoy this or that we lack so great and so true a good. For what is so present in the will as the will itself?"[107]

And in another passage I said, "Why do we think that we should doubt, even if we were never previously wise, that by our will we merit and live a praiseworthy and happy life, and by our will one that is base and wretched."[108]

Again, in another passage I said, "From this it follows that whoever wills to live uprightly and honestly, if he wills to will that in preference to fleeting things, obtains such a great thing with such great facility that to possess what he willed is nothing other than simply willing it."[109]

---

104. In his *Revisions* Augustine often refers to the Pelagians, whose position on grace he summarizes here, as "the recent heretics"(*novi heretici*, which also means "the new heretics"). There seems to be a hint of contempt in the expression, especially given the patristic reverence for antiquity and tradition in contrast to what is recent. See also *Revisions* I,9,4; 10,2; II,22,2; 33; 36; 53.
105. What follows is a series of passages from *Free Choice* in which Augustine acknowledges the role of the will without simultaneously acknowledging that of grace. He does not suggest that what he said needs to be corrected, although in sections 4-5 he adds other passages from the same work which affirm grace. This procedure—of exposition rather than revision—is exceptional in *The Revisions*.
106. I,1,1.
107. I,12,26.
108. I,13,28.
109. I,13,29.

Again, I said elsewhere, "For that eternal law, to the contemplation of which it is now time to return, has established this with an unwavering firmness: that there is merit in the will, but reward and punishment in happiness and wretchedness."[110]

And in another passage I said, "What anyone chooses to pursue and to embrace is located in the will."[111]

And in the second book I said, "For a man himself, to the degree that he is a man, is something good, because he can live uprightly when he wills."[112]

And in another passage I said, "There can be no upright behavior apart from this same free choice of will."[113]

And in the third book I said, "What need is there to investigate where this movement comes from, whereby the will turns away from an unchangeable good to a changeable good, since we acknowledge that it only comes from the soul and is voluntary and therefore culpable, and since every discipline that is useful in this regard is effective—once that movement has been condemned and checked—in turning our will away from a fall into temporal things to the enjoyment of an eternal good?"[114]

And in another passage I said, "It is truth that cries out most excellently in you. For you could not think that anything is in our power except that which we do when we will to do it. Hence nothing is so much in our own power as the will itself is. For, with no delay at all, it is there as soon as we will."[115]

Again, in another passage I said, "For, if you are praised for seeing what you ought to do, because you do not see it except in him who is unchangeable truth, how much more is he praised who has commanded the willing, bestowed the ability, and has not permitted a refusal to go unpunished?"[116] Then I said in ad-

110. I,14,30.
111. I,16,34.
112. II,1,2.
113. II,18,47.
114. III,1,2.
115. III,3,7.
116. III,16,46.

dition, "For, if everyone must do what he is equipped for, and if a person has been made in such a way that he necessarily sins, he must sin. When he sins, then, he does so because he must. If it is wicked to say this, then no one's nature forces him to sin."[117]

And again I said, "What, in the end, could be the will's cause before the will? For it is either the will itself, and one does not depart from that root which is the will, or it is not the will, and it has no sin. Either the will, therefore, is the first cause of sinning, or there is no sin that is the first cause of sinning. And there is no one to whom sin is rightfully imputed except the sinner. There is no one to whom it is rightfully imputed, then, except the one who wills it."[118]

And a little later I said, "Who sins in that which can in no way be avoided? But sin is committed; therefore it can be avoided."[119]

Pelagius used these statements of mine in a certain book of his. When I responded to that book, I wanted the title of my book to be *Nature and Grace*.[120]

4. Because God's grace, which was not an issue at the time, was not mentioned in these and similar words of mine, the Pelagians think, or could think, that we held their opinion. But in vain do they think this. The will, to be sure, is that by which one both sins and lives uprightly, which is what we were saying in those passages. The will itself, then, cannot be an upright and virtuous source of life for mortal men unless it is freed by God's grace from the slavery whereby it has become a slave of sin,[121] and is helped to overcome its vices. And this divine gift whereby it is freed would be given because of its merits and would not be grace, which is certainly freely given,[122] unless it [i.e., the divine gift] preceded

---

117. Ibid.
118. III,17,49.
119. III,18,50.
120. See *Revisions* II, 42. The title of Pelagius's book is never mentioned by Augustine, but it was most likely *Nature*.
121. See Rom 6:17, 20.
122. "Grace, which is certainly freely given": *gratia quae utique gratis datur.*

it. This we dealt with adequately in our other works,[123] when we refuted those enemies of this grace, the recent heretics.[124]

But even in these books on free choice, which were not at all written against them, because they did not yet exist, but were against the Manicheans, we were not entirely silent about that grace of God which, through their wicked impiousness, they attempt to abolish. For in the second book we said, "Not only the major but even the minor goods cannot exist unless they come from him from whom all good things come—that is, God."[125]

And shortly after that I said, "The virtues whereby one lives uprightly are major goods; the beauty of any bodies whatsoever, without which one can live uprightly, is a minor good; while the powers of the soul, without which one cannot live uprightly, are middle goods. No one uses virtues badly, but anyone can use the other goods—that is, the middle and the minor ones—not only well but also badly. And no one uses virtue badly because the work of virtue is the good use of those things that we can also use badly, but no one uses something badly by using it well. That is why the abundance and greatness of God's goodness has brought into existence not only the major goods but even the middle and the minor ones. His goodness is more praiseworthy in major goods than in middle ones, and more in middle ones than in minor ones, but more in all of them than if he had not bestowed all of them."[126]

And in another passage I said, "Hold onto your devotion so firmly that no good thing happens to you which you do not think or understand or in some way realize is from God."[127]

And again, in another passage I said, "But because man cannot also rise of his own accord as he fell of his own accord, let us with a firm faith grasp the hand of God that is stretched out to us from on high—that is, our Lord Jesus Christ."[128]

---

123. Augustine's anti-Pelagian writings are overwhelmingly concerned with the role of grace.
124. "The recent heretics": see p. 45, n. 104.
125. II,19,50.
126. Ibid.
127. II,20,54.
128. Ibid.

5. And in the third book I said something that Pelagius also made use of from my works. This is what I mentioned: "For who," I said, "sins in that which can in no way be avoided? But sin is committed; therefore it can be avoided."[129] Immediately after that I continued, "And yet even certain things done through ignorance are reproved and judged as requiring correction, as we read in the divine authorities. For the Apostle says, *I obtained mercy because I acted in ignorance* (1 Tm 1:13), and the prophet says, *Do not remember the crimes of my youth and of my ignorance* (Ps 24:7). There are also things done through necessity that must be reproved, when a person wills to act rightly and is unable to do so. That is the reason for these words: *For I do not do the good that I will, but the evil that I hate is what I do* (Rom 7:15). And these: *To will lies near at hand, but to accomplish the good does not* (Rom 7:18). And these: *The flesh lusts against the spirit, and the spirit against the flesh, for they are mutually opposed, so that you do not do the things that you will* (Gal 5:17). But all of these things pertain to human beings who are under the sentence of death. For, if this is not man's punishment but rather his nature, none of these things are sins. For, if there is no withdrawing from the way in which he was made by nature, such that he is unable to be better, when he does these things he is doing what he must. But if man were good, he would be different. But now, because he is the way he is, he is not good, and he does not have it in his power to be good, whether because he does not see what sort of person he should be, or because he sees and is unable to be the sort of person that he sees he should be. Who would doubt that this is a punishment? But every punishment, if it is just, is punishment for sin and is called a penalty.[130] If the punishment is unjust, however, since no one disputes the fact that it is a punishment, it has been imposed by some unjust person with higher authority. Yet, inasmuch as only a madman would

---

129. III,18,50.
130. "Punishment...penalty": *poena...supplicium.*

doubt the omnipotence and justice of God, this punishment is just and is connected with some sin. For no unjust ruler could snatch a person away from God as though he were unaware or tear him away against God's will as though he were powerless, either by frightening him or by contending with him, so that he might inflict an unjust punishment upon a person. The upshot, then, is that this punishment is just and results from man's condemnation."[131]

And in another passage I said, "To approve false things in place of true, so that a person may fall into error despite himself, and to be unable to restrain oneself from lascivious deeds because of the resistant and tormenting ache of the bonds of the flesh: this is not the nature of man as he was created but the punishment of one who has been condemned. But when we speak of a will that is free to act uprightly, we are speaking of that in which man was made."[132]

6. You can see how, long before the Pelagian heresy existed, we discussed these points as though we were already arguing with them. All good things were said to come from God—that is, the major and the middle and the minor—and the free choice of will is reckoned among middle goods, because we are also able to use it badly, but yet it is such that we are unable to live uprightly without it. The good use of it is a virtue that is discerned in major goods, which no one can use badly. And because, as has been said, all goods, the major and the middle and the minor, are from God, it follows that the good use of free will, which is a virtue and is numbered among the major goods, is also from God.

Then it is said that the grace of God frees a person from the wretchedness that is most justly inflicted on sinners, because of his own accord—that is, by free choice—he could fall and not also rise. To this wretchedness of a just condemnation belongs

131. III,18,51.
132. III,18,52.

the ignorance and misery that each human being suffers from the beginning of his birth, and no one is freed from this evil except by the grace of God. The Pelagians, who deny an original sin, do not want this wretchedness to proceed from a just condemnation. But even if ignorance and misery were part of man's primordial nature, God should not be blamed but praised for it, as we discussed in the same third book.[133]

This discussion is to be regarded as directed against the Manicheans, who do not accept the holy scriptures of the Old Testament,[134] in which there is an account of the original sin;[135] and whatever one may read about that in the apostolic writings [i.e., the New Testament] they insist with hateful impudence was inserted by corrupters of the scriptures, as though it had not been said by the apostles. Against the Pelagians, however, what both scriptures [i.e., the Old and New Testaments] speak of (which they profess to accept) must be defended.

This work begins in this way: "Tell me, I beseech you, whether God is the author of evil."

10 (9). Two Books On Genesis Against The Manicheans
(De Genesi Adversus Manichaeos Libri Duo)[136]

1. When I was now living in Africa, I wrote two books on Genesis against the Manicheans. It is true that whatever I discussed in previous books, when I showed that God was the supremely good and immutable creator of all mutable natures and that there was no evil nature or substance (to the degree that it is a nature and a substance), our thoughts were directed against the Manicheans. But these two books were published very explicitly against them in defense of the Old Law, which they oppose in the furious pur-

---

133. III,20,58; 22,65.
134. "Holy scriptures of the Old Testament": *scripturas sanctas veteris instrumenti.*
135. See Gn 3:1-6.
136. Written in 389.

suit of their insane error.[137] The first goes from what is written, *In the beginning God made heaven and earth* (Gn 1:1), up to when the seven days are completed, when we read that God rested on the seventh day.[138] The second goes from what is written, *This is the book of the creation of heaven and earth* (Gn 2:4), up to when Adam and his wife are sent out of paradise, and a guard is placed at the tree of life.[139] Finally, at the end of that book I distinguished the faith of Catholic truth from the error of the Manicheans, and I summarized in a succinct and clear fashion what they say and what we say.[140]

2. But regarding my words, "That light does not nourish the eyes of irrational birds but the pure hearts of those who believe in God and who turn away from the love of visible and temporal things to the fulfilling of his precepts, which all people are capable of if they will to be,"[141] the recent heretics, the Pelagians,[142] should not think that they were said in agreement with them. For it is entirely true that all people are capable of this if they will to be, but *the will is made ready by the Lord* (Prv 8:35 LXX), and by the gift of charity it is increased so much that they are capable, which was not said here because it was not pertinent to the matter at hand.

As to what is read there, that God's blessing, expressed in the words *Increase and multiply* (Gn 1:28), should be believed to have been directed toward fleshly fruitfulness after the sin,[143] I entirely disapprove if this cannot be seen as having had any other meaning than that those people would not have had children unless they sinned.

Also, regarding the green herbs and the fruit-bearing trees that are given as food to every kind of beast and to all birds and

---

137. See note 84.
138. See Gn 2:2-3.
139. See Gn 3:24.
140. II,24,37-29,43.
141. I,3,6.
142. "The recent heretics, the Pelagians": see p. 45, n.104.
143. I,19,30.

all serpents in the Book of Genesis,[144] inasmuch as there are both four-legged animals and birds that seem to live on flesh alone, it does not follow that this should be understood as having to be accepted exclusively in an allegorical sense.[145] For it could be that they would be fed by men from the fruits of the earth, if, because of the obedience with which men would serve God without any wickedness, they merited to have all the beasts and birds completely at their service.

Again, how I spoke of the people of Israel could also be confusing—"That people observed the law, even as far as bodily circumcision and sacrifices, as though they were in a sea of gentiles"[146]—since among the gentiles they had been unable to offer sacrifice, just as we see that now as well they have remained without sacrifices, unless perhaps the immolation of a lamb during Passover is understood as a sacrifice.[147]

3. In the second book also, when I said that the word *pabulum* could signify life,[148] it does not seem to have been said with sufficient aptness, since codexes with a better translation have not *pabulum* but *faenum*.[149] The word *faenum* does not correspond to the meaning "life" as *pabulum* does.

Again, I do not seem to have been correct in referring to what is written, *Why are earth and ashes proud?* (Sir 10:9), as prophetic words,[150] because they are not read in the book of someone who we are certain ought to be called a prophet.

Nor did I understand the words of the Apostle as he wished, where he uses a text from Genesis and says, *The first Adam was made into a living soul* (1 Cor 15:45), when I was explaining what was written, *God breathed into his face the breath of life, and the*

---

144. See Gn 1:30-31.
145. I,20,31.
146. I,23,40.
147. See *Answer to the Writings of Petilian* II,27,87.
148. II,3,4.
149. *Pabulum* is the Latin for "food," whereas *faenum* means "hay."
150. II,5,6.

man was made into a live soul, or *into a living soul* (Gn 2:7).[151] For the Apostle used this text in order to prove that the body was animal, whereas I thought that this was intended to show that man [i.e., man in his entirety], and not just man's body, was animal first.[152]

And when I said that "sins harm no one's nature but one's own,"[153] I said it because the one who harms a righteous person does not really harm him, when in fact his reward in heaven even increases,[154] but when he sins he really harms himself, because by the very will to do harm he will receive back the harm that he did. The Pelagians, to be sure, can make use of this statement, that "sins harm no one's nature but one's own," for their own teaching, and they can say that others' sins, then, have not harmed infants. Thus they give no thought to the fact that infants, who after all possess human nature, contract original sin, because human nature sinned in the first human beings, and that it is on this account that no sins but their own have harmed human nature. Through one man, indeed, in whom all sinned, sin entered into the world,[155] for I did not say that sins harm no man but rather "no one's nature but one's own."

Again, in what I said shortly after, that "no evil is natural,"[156] they can search for a hiding place in a similar way, except that what was said pertains to nature without vice, such as it was first created, for that is what is truly and properly called the nature of man. But in figurative language we also say that nature is how man is born.[157] That is how the Apostle spoke when he said, *For we too were once children of wrath by nature, just like the others* (Eph 2:3).

This work begins in this way: "If the Manicheans were to choose those whom they would deceive."

---

151. "Live...living": *vivam...viventem.*
152. II,8,10.
153. II,29,43.
154. See Mt 5:12; Lk 6:23.
155. See Rom 5:12.
156. II,29,43.
157. The Latin *natura* is related to the verb *nascor*, meaning "to be born." See also p. 72, n. 240.

11 (10). SIX BOOKS ON MUSIC
(De Musica Libri Sex)[158]

1. Then, as I mentioned previously,[159] I wrote six books on music. The sixth of these has become especially well known because the matter that it contains is worthy of reflection— how from bodily and spiritual but mutable numbers one may arrive at the immutable numbers that already exist in immutable truth itself, and thus *the invisible things of God may be seen and understood through things that have been made* (Rom 1:20).[160] Those who are incapable of this and nonetheless live by faith in Christ[161] come to the things that are to be seen in a more certain and happy way after this life. Those who are capable of it, however, if they lack faith in Christ, who is *the one mediator of God and men* (1 Tm 2:5), perish with all their wisdom.

2. In this book I said, "Bodies are better to the extent that they are more capable of being numbered by such numbers, but the soul becomes better by lacking those things that it receives through the body, when it turns itself away from the fleshly senses and is refashioned by the divine numbers of wisdom."[162] This must not be understood as though there were not going to be bodily numbers in incorruptible and spiritual bodies, when they are going to be much more beautiful and shapely, or as though the soul were not going to know them when it will be in its most excellent condition, as is the case when here [i.e., on earth] it becomes better by lacking them. For here it must turn away from the fleshly senses in order to seize upon intelligible realities, because it is weak and less capable of focusing upon both at the same time, and in these bodily

---

158. Begun in 387 and completed in its present state in 389. This was the only part of Augustine's project on the disciplines, or liberal arts, that he completed. See *Revisions* I,6.
159. See *Revisions* I,6.
160. The numbers (*numeri*) that are referred to here and elsewhere in this chapter can probably also be understood as rhythms or harmonies.
161. See Rom 1:17; 3:26; Gal 3:11; Heb 10:38.
162. VI,4,7.

things their allure must be guarded against now, as long as the soul can be seduced into base pleasure. But then it will be so firm and perfect that it will not be turned away by bodily numbers from the contemplation of wisdom, and it will know them in such a way as not to be seduced by them, and it will not become better by lacking them; but it will be so good and upright that they will be unable to be concealed from it or to take possession of it.

3. Again, I said, "This health will be most firm and assured when this body has been restored to its pristine stability at its proper time and in its proper order."[163] It ought not to be thought that this was said as though the bodies that will be in existence after the resurrection will not be better than those of the first human beings in paradise, because they [i.e., the post-resurrection bodies] will no longer need to be fed with the bodily foods with which they used to be fed; rather, this pristine stability should be taken to mean that those bodies will suffer no illness, just as they could not suffer it before the sin.

4. In another passage I said, "The love of this world is quite burdensome. For what the soul is seeking in it—namely, constancy and eternity—it does not find, because the lowest beauty achieves its end in the passing away of things, and that which imitates constancy in it is passed from the most high God through the soul, because beauty that is changeable in terms of time is superior to that which is changeable in terms of both time and place."[164] Clear reasoning defends these words if they can be taken in such a way that the lowest beauty is not understood except in regard to the bodies of men and of all ensouled beings that live with the senses of the body. What imitates constancy in that beauty is the fact that these same bodies maintain their structure (to the degree that they maintain it), and this is what is passed from the most high God through the soul. The soul possesses this very structure so that it may not be dissolved and disintegrate,

163. VI,5,13.
164. VI,14,44.

which is what we see happens in the bodies of ensouled beings when the soul departs. But if this lowest beauty is understood in terms of all bodies, that opinion demands believing that the world itself is also ensouled, so that what imitates constancy in it is passed from the most high God through its soul. But I have been unable to determine by any certain argument that this world is ensouled, as Plato thought, along with many other philosophers,[165] and I have not seen how I could be persuaded by the authority of the divine scriptures. Hence, I have noted as rashly stated something similar which could be taken in this way that was also said by me in the book on the immortality of the soul,[166] not because I declare that it is false but because I do not understand that it is true that the world is ensouled. Of course I do not doubt that this must be firmly adhered to—that this world is not God for us, whether it has a soul or not, because if it has one, he who made it is our God, whereas if it has none, it can be no one's god, much less ours. Yet, even if the world is not ensouled, it is most correctly believed, even by those who do not understand it, that there is a spiritual and vital power, and that this power serves God in the holy angels for the purpose of adorning and administering the world. At this point I wanted to call by the term "holy angels" every holy spiritual creature placed in God's secret and hidden service, but holy scripture is not accustomed to signify angelic spirits by the word "souls."[167]

Similarly, toward the end of this book I said, "The rational and intellectual numbers of the blessed and holy souls transmit the very law of God, apart from which a leaf does not fall from a tree and according to which our hairs have been numbered,[168] without the intervention of any nature, even to the courts of earth and hell."[169] I do not see how the word "souls" could be shown

165. See Plato, *Timaeus* 30b; Cicero, *De natura deorum* I,30.52; II,22.30.32.
166. See *The Immortality of the Soul* 15,24; *Revisions* I,5,3.
167. See also *Revisions* I,16,2.
168. See Mt 10:30 par.
169. VI,17,58.

to have been in keeping with the holy scriptures, since I wished only that the holy angels be understood here, and I do not recall having read anywhere in the divine writings that they have souls. This book begins in this way: "For too long a time."[170]

12 (11). One Book On The Teacher
(De Magistro Liber Unus)[171]

During the same period I wrote a book entitled *On the Teacher*, in which there is discussed and sought and found[172] that there is no teacher except God who teaches man knowledge, in accordance with what is written in the gospel: *One is your teacher, the Christ* (Mt 23:10).

This book begins in this way: "What do we seem to you to wish to accomplish when we speak?"

13 (12). One Book On True Religion
(De Vera Religione Liber Unus)[173]

1. Then I also wrote a book on true religion, in which it is discussed in a many-faceted and lengthy way that the one true God—that is, the Trinity of Father and Son and Holy Spirit—should be worshiped by the true religion; and with what great mercy on his part the Christian religion, which is the true religion, has been vouchsafed to men over the course of the temporal dispensation; and how man should be made fit by a certain gentleness[174] for this same worship of God. Yet this book speaks in particular against the two natures of the Manicheans.[175]

---

170. Since Augustine has chosen not to discuss all six books of this work but only the sixth, by way of exception he cites the first words of the sixth book rather than those at the beginning of the entire treatise.
171. Written in 389.
172. This triad corresponds roughly to Mt 7:7-8 par.
173. Written between the end of 389 and the beginning of 390.
174. Reading *quadam suavitate* instead of *quadam sua vita.*
175. See p. 38, n. 76.

2. In a certain passage of this book I said, "It should be clear and evident to you that there could be no error in religion if, in place of its God, the soul did not worship a soul or a body or its own imaginings."[176] Here I used "soul" for every incorporeal creature. I was not speaking as the scriptures do; when they do not use some figurative term or other, they only wish that to be understood which causes mortal ensouled beings to live, including human beings, inasmuch as they are mortal. Shortly after that, though, I captured the same meaning better and more briefly when I said, "Let us not, then, serve creation rather than the creator,[177] nor let us fade away in our own thoughts,[178] and that is perfect religion."[179] I signified the twofold creation—that is, spiritual and bodily—by a single word.[180] In addition I said "or its own imaginings" in the former place, which is why I said here "nor let us fade away in our own thoughts."

3. Again, I said, "That is, in our time, the Christian religion; to know it and to follow it is the safest and most certain salvation."[181] This was said in keeping with the name and not in keeping with the reality itself that is designated by the name. For the reality itself, which is now called the Christian religion, also existed among the ancients, and it was not absent from the beginning of the human race up until Christ himself came in the flesh.[182] It was then that the true religion, which already existed, began to be referred to as Christian. For when, after the resurrection and the ascension into heaven, the apostles had begun to preach him and many believed, the disciples, as it is written, were called Chris-

176. 10,18.
177. See Rom 1:25.
178. See Rom 1:21.
179. 10,19.
180. I.e., "creation." The Latin *creatura* could as well be translated here either "creation" or "creature," "creation" suggesting the whole of creation or the act of creation, and "creature" suggesting an individual created being, although neither excludes the other.
181. Ibid.
182. That the Church, and hence Christians, existed even before the coming of Christ is an idea that can be traced back at least as far as the second century. See, e.g., Justin, *1 Apology* 46; *2 Clement* 14. And for Augustine see also *The Perfection of Human Righteousness* 19, 42.

tians for the first time in Antioch.[183] That is why I said, "This is, in our time, the Christian religion," not because in previous times it did not exist but because in later times it received this name.

4. In another passage I said, "Pay attention, then, to the things that follow, and do so in a careful and devout way, as much as you can, for God helps such persons."[184] This ought not to be understood as though he helps only such persons, since he also helps those who are not such so that they may be such—that is, so that they may seek in a careful and devout way, and such he helps so that they may find.[185]

Again, I said elsewhere, "Then what follows will be that, after the bodily death that we owe to the first sin, this body will be restored, in its own time and in its own order, to its pristine stability."[186] This should be understood in such a way that the body's pristine stability, which we lost by sinning, will also have such great happiness that it will not yield to the decline of old age. This body will be restored to this pristine stability, then, in the resurrection of the dead. But it will possess it more abundantly, so that it will not be sustained by bodily food but will be given life in sufficiency by the spirit alone when it has risen as a life-giving spirit,[187] and for that reason it will be spiritual as well. That which came first, however, although it would not have died if the man had not sinned, was nonetheless made animal—that is, made into a living soul.[188]

5. And elsewhere I said, "To such an extent is sin a voluntary evil that it is in no way sin if it is not voluntary."[189] This explanation can appear false, but, if it is carefully examined, it will be found to be quite true. That should be considered sin which is sin alone, not what is also the punishment for sin, as I showed previously,

183. See Acts 11:26.
184. 10,20.
185. See Mt 7:7-8 par.
186. 12,25.
187. See 1 Cor 15:45.
188. See Gn 2:7. "Made animal...living soul": *animale factum est...in animam viventem.*
189. 14,27.

when I was recalling some things from the third book of *Free Choice*.[190] There are also sins that not without reason are referred to as involuntary, because they are perpetrated in ignorance or under compulsion. Yet they can never be committed apart from the will, since even one who sins in ignorance is certainly doing so[191] by means of his will, because, although it is something that should not be done, he thinks that it should be done, and he whose flesh desires against the spirit[192] does not do what he wills; indeed, he desires unwillingly, and in that respect he does not do what he wills. But, if he is overcome, he consents willingly to the desire, and in that respect he only does what he wills, as someone free of righteousness and enslaved to sin.[193] And what is called original sin in infants, when they still do not have use of the choice of their will, is not absurdly called voluntary as well, because it was contracted from the first bad will of man and in some way became hereditary. And so what I said—"To such an extent is sin a voluntary evil that it is in no way sin if it is not voluntary"—is not false. Therefore by God's grace not only is the guilt of all past [sins] absolved in all those who are baptized in Christ, which is brought about by the Spirit of regeneration, but also in adults the will itself is cleansed and equipped by the Lord, which is brought about by a spirit of faith and charity.

6. In another passage, when I said of the Lord Jesus Christ, "He accomplished nothing by force but everything by persuasion and admonition," it had not occurred to me that he drove the buyers and sellers out of the Temple with a whip.[194] But what does this matter (although in fact he also drove demons against their will out of people not by persuasive words but by the force of his power[195])?

Again, in another passage I said, "The first ones who ought to be followed are those who say that the one, highest and unique

190. See *Revisions* I,9,5.
191. Reading *facit* instead of *peccat*.
192. See Gal 5:17.
193. See Rom 6:20.
194. See Jn 2:14-16.
195. See Mt. 9:32, etc.

and true God[196] must be worshiped. If the truth does not shine out from them, only then must they be abandoned."[197] It can seem that I said this as though I doubted the truth of this religion. But I spoke in a way that corresponded to the person to whom I was writing.[198] For I spoke thus, "If the truth does not shine out from them," not doubting that it *was* shining out from them, just as the Apostle said, *If Christ has not risen* (1 Cor 15:14), not in the least doubting that he *did* rise.

7. Again, I said, "Those miracles have not been permitted to continue until our own times, lest the soul always be seeking visible realities and the human race grow cold through being accustomed to things whose novelty attracted it."[199] This is certainly true, for, when the hand is being imposed upon those who have been baptized, they no longer receive the Holy Spirit in such a way as to speak with the tongues of all the nations,[200] nor are the sick healed now by the mere shadow of Christ's preachers as they pass by,[201] and if such things were done in that way then, it is evident that since then they have ceased. But what I said should not be understood as though no miracles should be believed to be performed nowadays in Christ's name. For I myself, when I was writing this very book, knew a blind man who had been given his sight in the same city near the bodies of the martyrs of Milan.[202] I knew of some other miracles as well; so many of them occur even in these times that we would be unable either to be aware of all of them or to number those of which we are aware.[203]

---

196. Reading *unum summum et solum et verum Deum* instead of *unum Deum summum, solum, verum Deum et solum.*
197. 25,46.
198. This person was Romanianus, a friend and benefactor of Augustine's. See 7,12; Letter 15,1.
199. Ibid.
200. See Acts 2:4; 10:46.
201. See Acts 5:15.
202. These were the martyrs Gervase and Protase. The miracle was a famous one and is mentioned in *Confessions* IX,7,16; *The City of God* XXII,8; Sermon 286,4; Ambrose, Letter 22; Paulinus of Milan, *The Life of Saint Ambrose* 14.
203. See *The City of God* XXII,8. And see as well *Revisions* I,14,5, where Augustine also speaks of contemporary miracles but is more modest in suggesting how many there are.

8. And what I said in another place, "As the Apostle says, 'All order is from God,'"[204] the Apostle did not say in the same words, although the sense appears to be the same. What he actually said was, *The things that exist have been ordained by God* (Rom 13:1). And elsewhere I said, "Let no one at all deceive us. Whatever is rightly censured is rejected by comparison with what is better."[205] This was said about substances and natures, for that was what was being discussed, not about good actions and sins.

Again, I said elsewhere, "One man ought not to be loved by another man as blood brothers are loved, or children, or spouses, or kinsfolk, or neighbors, or fellow citizens, because that love is temporal. For we would not have any such relationships, which arise through being born and through dying, if our nature remained in the commandments and the image of God and was not thrust into this corruption."[206] I utterly reject this opinion, which I already previously rejected in the first book of *On Genesis against the Manicheans.*[207] It leads to the belief that that first couple were not going to beget descendents unless they sinned, as though it had been necessary that they would be begotten destined to die if they were begotten of the coupling of that husband and wife. For I had not yet seen that it could have been the case that those who were not going to die might be born from those who were not going to die, had not human nature been changed for the worse because of that great sin, and thus, if in both parents and children fruitfulness and bliss had continued, human beings would have been born—up to the fixed number of saints that God predestined[208]—not as those who were going to succeed their dying parents but as those who were going to reign with living ones. Those relations and kinships would also exist, then, if no one did wrong and no one died.

---

204. 41,77.
205. 41,78.
206. 46,88.
207. See *Revisions* I,10,2.
208. See Rev 14:1-3 (?); Rom 8:28-30; Eph 1:5.12.

9. Again, in another passage I said, "Striving towards the one God and binding our souls (which supposedly gives its name to religion[209]) to him who is one, let us abandon all superstition."[210] The reason that was given in these words of mine for the origin of the word "religion" was the one that pleased me more. For it does not escape me that authors of the Latin language have given another explanation for the origin of this word, which is that "religion" is so called from the fact that it is gathered together again. This word is taken from "selecting"—that is, "choosing"—so that in Latin "gather together again" seems to be the same as "choose."[211]

This book begins in this way: "Since the path of every good and happy life."

14 (13). ONE BOOK ADDRESSED TO HONORATUS ON THE ADVANTAGE OF BELIEVING

(De Utilitate Credendi Ad Honoratum Liber Unus)[212]

1. When I was now a presbyter at Hippo Regius I wrote a book on the advantage of believing to a friend of mine who had been deceived by the Manicheans. I knew that he was still being held captive by that error and was making fun of the teaching of the Catholic faith, because people were commanded to believe but were not taught what was true by the surest reasoning.

In this book I said, "But in some precepts and commandments of the law, which it is not now permissible for a Catholic to observe,

---

209. "Binding...religion": *religantes...religio.*
210. 55,111.
211. "Is gathered together again...selecting...choosing...gather together again... choose": *religitur...legendo...eligendo...religo...eligo.* The explanation as Augustine cites it is found in Cicero, *De natura deorum* II,28,72, where a distinction is made between the superstitious and the religious. "Those who carefully reconsidered and as it were gathered together again everything that pertained to the worship of the gods are called religious from 'gathering together again' (*relegendo*)."
212. Written between early 391 and August 392. Honoratus, who is described as having been deceived by the Manicheans, was one of a number of Augustine's friends who had embraced Manicheanism, and he was apparently the only one remaining who had not rejected it in favor of Christianity. He is often identified with the Honoratus for whom Augustine wrote *The Grace of the New Testament.* See *Revisions* II,36.

whether it be such a thing as the sabbath or circumcision or sacrifices or anything else of the sort, such great mysteries are contained that every devout person understands that nothing is more destructive than accepting something in them according to the letter—that is, according to the word—and that nothing is more beneficial than that it be disclosed by the Spirit. That is why *the letter kills, but the spirit gives life* (2 Cor 3:6)."[213] But I have explained those words of the apostle Paul in another way and—as far as I can tell, or, rather, as is apparent from the things themselves—much more suitably in the book that is entitled *The Spirit and the Letter*,[214] although this understanding is also not to be rejected.

2. Again, I said, "There are two praiseworthy persons in religion. One belongs to those who have already found, who must also be considered the happiest; the other belongs to those who most zealously and uprightly seek. [215] The first, then, are already in actual possession; the others are on the path by which they will most certainly arrive."[216] If those who, in these words of mine, have already found, who I said were in actual possession, are held to be the happiest in such a way as not to be so in this life but are such in the one for which we hope and to which we are journeying along faith's path, then this understanding is not erroneous. For they are to be considered as having found what was to be sought for, and they are already where we desire to arrive by seeking and believing—that is, by staying on faith's path. But if they are thought to be, or to have been, such in this life, it does not seem to me to be true, not because in this life absolutely nothing true can be found that is discerned by the mind rather than believed by faith but because, whatever it is, it is not enough to confer the utmost happiness. It is not as though what the Apostle refers to when he says, *We see now through a mirror in obscurity*, and *Now I know partly* (1 Cor 13:12), is not seen by the mind. Of course it is seen, but it is not enough to confer the greatest happiness. What

213. 3,9.
214. See *The Spirit and the Letter* 5,7.
215. See Mt 7:7-8 par.
216. 11,25.

makes for the greatest happiness is what he says: *But then face to face*, and *Then I shall know as I have been known* (1 Cor 13:12). Those who have found this must be said to be abiding in the possession of happiness, which the path of faith to which we are adhering leads us to, and where we desire to arrive by believing. But who those happiest ones are, who are already in possession of what this path leads to, is a great question. To be sure, there is no question that the holy angels are there. But whether at least those holy human beings who are now dead should be said to abide in its possession is worth investigating. For now they have in fact been stripped of the corruptible body that weighs down the soul,[217] but they themselves also await the redemption of their body,[218] and their flesh reposes in hope[219] and does not yet shine with its coming incorruptibility. But whether, because of this, given that it says *face to face*, they will be less capable of contemplating the truth with the eyes of their heart, is not something that we can discuss and examine here.

Again, what I said, "For the happiest thing is to know what is great and good or even divine,"[220] we must refer to that same happiness. For in this life, however much something may be known, it still does not confer the most happiness, because what is as yet unknown is incomparably greater.

3. And I said, "There is a great difference between what is grasped by the mind's sure reasoning, which we call knowing, and what is beneficially passed on to our descendents by way of the spoken or written word as something that must be believed."[221] And shortly thereafter I said, "What we know, then, we owe to reason, what we believe to authority."[222] This must not be understood in such a way that, when speaking casually, we would be afraid of saying that we know something because we believe suitable wit-

---

217. See Wis 9:15.
218. See Rom 8:23.
219. See Ps 15:9.
220. 11,25.
221. Ibid.
222. Ibid.

nesses. To be sure, when we speak properly, we say that we only know what we understand with the mind's firm reasoning. But when we speak in a way that corresponds more to common usage, which is how divine scripture also speaks, we should not hesitate to say that we know both what we perceive with the senses of our body and what we believe through faith by means of worthy witnesses, as long as we understand, however, what the difference is between the one and the other.

4. Again, what I said, "No one doubts that all human beings are either foolish or wise,"[223] can seem to contradict what one reads in the third book of *Free Choice*: "It is as though human nature admits no intermediate condition apart from foolishness and wisdom."[224] But that was said in that passage when there was a question about the first man, whether he was created wise or foolish or neither, because in no way were we able to call a person foolish who was created without defect, given that foolishness is a great defect, and it was not very clear how we could call a person wise who was capable of being led astray. Hence I tried to express the matter briefly by saying, "It is as though human nature admits no intermediate condition apart from foolishness and wisdom." Indeed, I saw that we also cannot say that infants, who we profess have contracted original sin but who do not yet make use of free choice either well or badly, are either wise or foolish. But I said at this point that all human beings were either wise or foolish— meaning those who already have the use of reason, whereby human beings are distinguished from beasts—just as we say that all human beings want to be happy. Do we fear that in these words, which are so plain and clear, infants (who are as yet incapable of wanting this) would also be understood?

5. In another passage, when I was mentioning the miracles that the Lord Jesus performed when he was here in the flesh, I added this and said, "Why, you ask, do these things not happen nowadays?" And I replied, "Because they would not be striking unless they were

---

223. 12,27.
224. *Free Choice* III,24,71.

marvelous, but if they were familiar occurrences they would not be marvelous."[225] I said this because there are not such great nor so many [miracles] nowadays, not because none happen nowadays.[226]

6. At the end of the book I said, "But because these words of ours have gone on much longer than I thought, let us end this book here. My wish is that you will remember that in it I did not yet begin to refute the Manicheans and did not yet attack that nonsense or disclose anything of importance about the Catholic Church[227] itself. Instead I only wanted to rescue you, if I could, from a false opinion that was taught to us, whether maliciously or ignorantly, concerning true Christians, and to lift you up to learn certain great and divine things. That is why this volume is the way it is. Once your feelings are somewhat calmed down, I shall perhaps be readier for other things."[228] I did not say this as though up until then I had written nothing against the Manicheans or had committed to writing nothing about Catholic teaching, since so many previously published volumes attest that I was not silent about either topic. But in this book, which was written for that man, I had not yet begun to refute the Manicheans and had not yet attacked that nonsense, nor had I disclosed anything of importance about the Catholic Church itself, because I was hoping that, once I had begun in this way, I was going to write to him what I had not yet written here.

This book begins in this way: "If it seemed to me to be one and the same thing, Honoratus."

225. 16,34.
226. See *Revisions* I,13,7 and p. 62, n. 203.
227. "Catholic Church": *catholica*. This was one of Augustine's favorite ways of referring to the Church. See also *Revisions* II,18; 25; and p. 125, n. 65.
228. 18,36.

15 (14). One Book Against The Manicheans On The Two Souls

(De Duabus Animabus Contra Manichaeos Liber Unus)[229]

1. After this book, while I was still a presbyter, I wrote against the Manicheans on the two souls. They say that one of them is a part of God and that the other is from the nation of darkness, which God did not create and which is coeternal with God. And they rave that both these souls, one good and the other bad, exist in a single person. The bad one they say belongs to the flesh, and they also say that the flesh belongs to the nation of darkness; the good one, however, is from an adventitious part of God that struggled with the nation of darkness and mingled the two. And in fact they attribute everything good in a person to that good soul, but everything bad to that bad soul.

In this book I said, "There is no life of whatever sort which, for the very reason that it is life, and insofar as it is life at all, does not belong to the highest font and source of life."[230] I spoke in this way so that creation would be understood to belong to the creator, but not so that it would be thought that he was a part of it.

2. Again, I said, "Nowhere is there sin unless it is in the will."[231] The Pelagians could think that this was said in agreement with them in respect to infants, who they deny have the sin that is forgiven them in baptism, because they do not yet have the use of the choice of the will. This is like saying that the sin which we say they derived originally from Adam (that is, they are involved in its guilt, and because of that they are considered liable to punishment) could exist somewhere else than in the will, by which will it was committed when the transgression of the divine precept occurred. This statement, where we said, "Nowhere is there sin unless it is in

---

229. Written between 391 and 395.
230. 1,1,
231. 9,12.

the will," can also be thought to be false because the Apostle said, *But if I do that which I do not will, it is no longer I who do it, but that sin which dwells in me* (Rom 7:20). For so little is this sin in the will that he says, *I do that which I do not will*. How, then, is sin nowhere except in the will? But this sin, which the Apostle spoke about as he did, is called sin because it was brought about by sin and is the punishment for sin, since this is said about the concupiscence of the flesh. This is clear from what he says in what follows, *I know that the good does not dwell in me, that is, in my flesh; for to will lies near at hand, but to accomplish the good does not* (Rom 7:18). It is certainly the perfection of the good person that the very desire for sin, to which the will in fact does not consent when one lives well, not be in a person. But he does not accomplish the good because there is still in him the concupiscence that the will resists. The guilt of this concupiscence is absolved in baptism, but the weakness remains, which each believer who is making good progress most earnestly struggles against until he is healed. But the sin that is nowhere except in the will is chiefly to be understood as that which a just condemnation has followed, for *it entered into the world through one man* (Rom 5:12). Yet this sin as well, whereby consent is given to the desire for sin, is not committed except by way of the will. Hence I also said in another passage, "There is no sin, then, except by way of the will."[232]

3. And again, in another passage I defined the will itself and said, "The will is the movement of the mind, under no compulsion, either not to lose something or else to acquire something."[233] This was said for the purpose of drawing a distinction, by way of this definition, between willing and not willing. Thus intention would be attributed to those who, as the first ones in paradise, were the source of evil for the human race. They were under no compulsion to sin—that is, to sin by free will, for they knowingly acted against the precept, and the tempter persuaded them to do this but did not

---

232. 10,14.
233. Ibid.

compel them.[234] The person who has sinned unknowingly can not inappropriately be said to have sinned unwillingly, although he still willingly did what he did unknowingly, and so there could be no sin without his will. This will, as it was defined, "is the movement of the mind, under no compulsion, either not to lose something or else to acquire something." If he had not willed it, he would not have done it; he was not compelled to do it. Because he willed it, he therefore did it, even if he did not sin because he willed it, not knowing that it was sin that he did. Hence even such sin cannot exist without the will, but by willing the deed and not by willing the sin; this deed, nonetheless, was a sin, for this deed is something that ought not to have been done. Whoever sins knowingly, on the other hand, if, without sinning, he is able to resist what is compelling him to sin and still does not do so, certainly sins willingly, because one who is able to resist is not compelled to yield. But one who is unable, by means of a good will, to resist a compelling desire and therefore acts against the precepts of righteousness—this is a sin in such a way that it is also punishment for the sin. On this account it is most true that there can be no sin without the will.

4. Again, I gave a definition of sin when I said, "Sin is the will to hold fast to or to pursue what righteousness forbids, and from which one is free to abstain."[235] This is true because what is defined is only what sin is, not also what the punishment for sin is. For when it is such that it is also the punishment for sin, how much power does the will have under a domineering desire except, perhaps, if it is devout, to pray for help? For it is free to the extent that it has been freed, and to that extent it is called will. Otherwise will must properly be called utter desire, which is not, as the Manicheans rave, the addition of a foreign nature but a defect of our own of which we are not healed except by the Savior's grace. If anyone says that this desire is nothing else than the will, although vicious and enslaved to sin, he ought not to be

---

234. See Gn 3:1-6.
235. 11,15. See *Unfinished Work in Answer to Julian* I,44-45.104.

contradicted, and there ought to be no argument over the words, since the truth of the matter is clear. In this way too it is evident that there is no sin without the will, whether in act or in origin.

5. Again, I said there, "I was still able to ask whether that evil kind of soul, before being mixed with the good, had any will. For if it did not have one, it was sinless and innocent and therefore not at all evil."[236] Why, then, they ask, do you speak of a sin of infants, whose will you do not consider guilty?[237] The response is that they are considered guilty not because of possessing a will but because of their origin. For, in terms of origin, what is every earthly human being but Adam? Adam certainly had a will, however, and, when he sinned by that will, sin entered into the world through him.[238]

6. Again, I said, "Souls cannot in any way be evil by nature."[239] If there is a question as to how we would understand what the Apostle says, *We ourselves were by nature children of wrath, just like the others* (Eph 2:3), we respond that I wished nature, in these words of mine, to be understood as that which is properly called nature, in which we were created without vice. For this is called nature on account of our origin,[240] and this origin has a defect, to be sure, which is against nature.

And again I said, "That someone should be considered guilty of sin because he did not do what he could not do is the height of wickedness and insanity."[241] Why, then, they say, are infants considered guilty?[242] The response should be that they are considered such from the origin of him who did not do what he could do—namely, observe the divine mandate.

I said, "Whatever those souls do, if they do it by nature and not by will (that is, if they lack free movement of mind both to

---

236. 12,16.
237. Augustine is reflecting the thought of the Pelagians, who denied original sin and its effects in infants.
238. See Rom 5:12.
239. 12,17.
240. The Latin *natura* is related to the verb *nascor*, which means "to be born." To be born means to originate, and hence the connection between nature and origin.
241. 13,20.
242. The question is one that Pelagians would ask.

act and not to act, and if the ability to refrain from their activity is not granted them), we cannot consider to be a sin of theirs."[243] The question about infants is not problematic here, because they are considered guilty on account of the origin of him who sinned by will, when he was not lacking free movement of mind both to act and not to act, and he had the greatest ability to refrain from doing evil. The Manicheans do not say this about the nation of darkness, which they bring up in the most far-fetched manner, and they insist that its nature was always evil and never good.

7. There could also be a question as to what I meant when I said, "Even if there are souls given over to bodily tasks not by sin but by nature (which for the time being is uncertain), and, although they are inferior, they are connected to us through some inner proximity, they must not be considered evil because we, when we pursue and love bodily things, are evil."[244] I said this about those [souls] of which I had begun to speak previously, when I said, "Although, even if it is conceded to these same persons [i.e., the Manicheans] that we are drawn to base things by another inferior kind of soul, they do not therefore cause either the ones to be evil by nature or the others to be the highest good."[245] From here I prolonged the discussion as far as the passage where I said, "Even if there are souls given over to bodily tasks not by sin but by nature (which for the time is being uncertain)," and so forth. The question could be asked, then, as to why I said "which for the time being is uncertain," since I should by no means have doubted that such souls do not exist. I said this, though, because I have known from experience persons who said that the devil and his angels are good in their kind and in the nature in which God created them such as they are, in their proper order, but that they are an evil for us if we are led astray and seduced by them, while, if we are wary of them and overcome them, they are something beautiful and glorious. And those who say this think that they use

243. 13,20.
244. 13,20.
245. 13,20.

suitable proof texts from scripture to demonstrate it—either what is written in the Book of Job, when the devil is described, *This is the beginning of the Lord's work, which he made to be mocked by his angels* (Jb 40:19 LXX), or what is in Psalm 103, *This serpent which you fashioned to make a mockery of him* (Ps 104:26). This question, which should not have been taken up and answered in response to the Manicheans, who do not think this, but in response to others who do think it, I did not wish to examine and untangle at the time, lest I write a much longer book than I wanted to. For I saw that, even if this point were conceded, the Manicheans still had to be and now could be refuted when, through a most insane error, they introduced a nature of evil that was coeternal with the eternal good. And so I said "which for the time being is uncertain" not because I myself had doubts about the matter but because, between me and those who I had discovered thought this way, the question was not yet resolved. Nonetheless, in my books on the literal meaning of Genesis, written long after, I resolved as much of it as I could through an exegesis of the holy scriptures.[246]

8. In another passage I said, "We sin by loving bodily things because we are commanded by justice to love spiritual things and are able to do so by nature, and it is then that we are best and happiest in our kind."[247] Here it can be asked why I said that we are able to do so by nature and not by grace. But it was a question concerning nature that was raised in response to the Manicheans. To be sure, grace brings it about that nature, once it has been healed, is, *through him who came to seek and to save what was perishing* (Lk 19:10), able to do what it cannot do when it is subject to vice. I recall that even then I prayed for this grace for those closest to me who were still held by that deathly error, and I said, "Great God, almighty God, God of the highest goodness, who it is right to believe and understand is inviolable and immutable, Threefold Unity, whom the Catholic Church worships, I, who have experienced your mercy towards me, humbly pray

---

246. See *The Literal Meaning of Genesis* XI,13,17-25,33.
247. 13,20.

that you will not allow the men with whom I lived in complete agreement in all our life together, from my youth up, to disagree with me in your worship."²⁴⁸ Praying in this way I already grasped by faith not only that those who have turned to God are helped by his grace to advance and to become perfect, when it can still be said that this grace is given in accord with the merit of their conversion, but also that it is by this very grace of God that they turn to God. Then I prayed for those who were utterly turned away from him, and I prayed that they would be turned to him.

This book begins in this way: "With the help of God's mercy."

16 (15). The Acts Of A Debate With Fortunatus, A Manichean, In One Book

*(Acta Contra Fortunatum Manichaeum, Liber Unus)*²⁴⁹

1. At the same time during my presbyterate I had a debate with a certain Fortunatus, a presbyter of the Manicheans, who had lived a long time at Hippo and had led so many astray that, because of them, he enjoyed living there. As we were arguing back and forth this debate was taken down in writing by notaries, as though official acts were being composed, for it lists both the day and the consul. We saw to it that this was put into a book that would be available to posterity. The question discussed here is where evil comes from. I asserted that human evil had its origin in the free choice of the will, while he strove to advance the idea that the nature of evil was coeternal with God. But on the next day he finally admitted that he could find nothing to say against us. He did not become a Catholic, to be sure, but he did leave Hippo.

2. In this book I said, "I say that the soul was made by God just like everything else that was made by God, and, among the things that almighty God made, the principal place has been giv-

---

248. 15,24.
249. This debate was held August 28-29, 392. The fifth day before the Kalends of September, cited at the beginning of the work, is August 28ᵗʰ. For another brief reference to Fortunatus see *Revisions* II,8.

en to the soul."[250] I spoke like this with the wish that it be taken generally as referring to the entire rational creation, although in the holy scriptures the souls of angels either are not spoken of at all or this cannot easily be discovered, as we have already said previously.[251]

Again, in another passage I said, "I say that there is no sin unless a sin is committed by one's own will."[252] There I wanted that sin to be understood which is not also punishment for sin. Elsewhere in the same debate I said what needed to be said about punishment of that sort.

And again, I said that "that very same flesh, which tormented us with punishments while we abided in our sins, would afterwards be subject to us in the resurrection, and it would not make it difficult for us to observe the law and the divine precepts."[253] This must not be understood as though even in the kingdom of God, where we shall have an incorruptible and immortal body, the law and the precepts from the divine scriptures would have to be maintained, but because the eternal law will be observed there perfectly, and we shall keep those two precepts of love of God and neighbor[254] not by reading but by perfect and everlasting love itself.

This work begins in this way: "On the fifth day before the Kalends of September, when Arcadius Augustus (for the second time) and Rufinus, most illustrious men, were consuls."

17 (16). ONE BOOK ON FAITH AND THE CREED
(De Fide Et Symbolo Liber Unus)[255]

During the same period, in the presence of the bishops who ordered me to do this and who were holding a plenary council

---

250. 1,13.
251. See *Revisions* I,11,4.
252. 1,15.
253. 2,22.
254. See Mt 22:37-39 par.
255. This talk was delivered October 8, 393, when the plenary council that is mentioned in the text was being held. The Latin *symbolum*, taken from the Greek, was an ancient and well-established term for "creed" or "profession of faith."

of all of Africa[256] at Hippo Regius, I gave a talk as a presbyter on faith and the creed.[257] I turned this talk into a book at the very eager insistence of several of them with whom I was quite close. In it the discussion of these things is carried out in such a way as not to reproduce the text of the words which is given to the *competentes* to be memorized. [258]

In this book, when the subject was the resurrection of the flesh, I said, "According to the Christian faith, which cannot be mistaken, the body will rise. This seems incredible to someone who is aware of what the flesh is now but does not consider what it will be, because at that time of angelic transformation it will no longer be flesh and blood but only body," and so forth.[259] I said this then about the transformation of earthly bodies into heavenly bodies because, when the Apostle was speaking about this, he said, *Flesh and blood will not possess the kingdom of God* (1 Cor 15:50). But whoever understands these words so as to think that the earthly body, as we now have it, will be changed into a heavenly body by the resurrection, in such a way that neither its members nor the substance of the flesh will exist, must certainly be corrected and made to recall the body of the Lord, who, after rising with the same members, appeared not only visible to the eye but even touchable by the hand, and he made it clear that he possessed flesh when he said, *Touch and see that a spirit does not have bones and flesh as you see that I have* (Lk 24:39). Hence it is obvious that the Apostle did not deny that the substance of the flesh will exist

---

256. "All of Africa" refers to the area whose administrative center was Carthage.
257. An address by a presbyter to a council of bishops would have been a rarity at the time; it attests to Augustine's reputation that he was asked to speak at such an event. It is perhaps also a reflection on the educational level of the bishops to whom he was speaking that Aurelius, who had invited him, had asked him to talk on so rudimentary a topic as the creed. See J. E. Merdinger, *Rome and the African Church in the Time of Augustine* (New Haven 1997) 72.
258. The *competentes* were those who were being prepared for baptism. Augustine refers to the fact that, a few weeks before their baptism, the creed was given to them to be memorized. Although he deals with the articles of the creed in their classical order, Augustine does not cite them verbatim, which is probably what he is alluding to when he says that the wording was not presented in the way with which the *competentes* would have been familiar.
259. 10,24.

in the kingdom of God but that by the term *flesh and blood* he referred either to persons who live according to the flesh or to the very corruption of the flesh, which will certainly not exist then. For when he said, *Flesh and blood will not possess the kingdom of God*, what he said immediately after is rightly understood to have been added as an explanation: *Neither will corruption possess incorruption* (1 Cor 15:50). Whoever reads the final book of *The City of God*[260] will see that I discussed this difficult matter as carefully as I could with the intention of persuading unbelievers.

This book begins in this way: "Because it is written."

18 (17). ONE BOOK OF AN UNFINISHED LITERAL COMMENTARY ON GENESIS
(De Genesi Ad Litteram Imperfectus Liber Unus)[261]

Since, when I had composed the two books on Genesis against the Manicheans, I had treated the words of scripture in accordance with their allegorical meaning, I did not venture to give a literal explanation of all the secrets of natural things—that is, how what was said there could be understood in keeping with its historical character. In this very arduous and difficult work as well I wanted to get a sense of what I was capable of, but in the course of explaining the scriptures my inexperience was overcome by this burdensome effort, and when one book had not yet been completed I withdrew from a task that I was unable to sustain. While I was engaged in revising my writings, this very [book],[262] incomplete as it was, fell into my hands. I had not published it and had ordered its destruction, because afterwards I wrote twelve books entitled *The Literal Meaning of Genesis*. Although there seem to be many more questions raised than answers found in them, yet this one[263] must not be compared with them. After I revised it, however, I

---

260. See *The City of God* XXII,5.21.
261. Written between 393 and 395.
262. "This very [book]": *iste ipse*. The Latin pronoun *iste* often has a derogatory connotation.
263. *Iste*—i.e., the *Unfinished Literal Commentary on Genesis*.

wanted to keep it so that there would be an indication, which I thought might not be useless, of my early attempts at clarifying and examining the divine writings, and I wanted it to be entitled *An Unfinished Literal Commentary on Genesis*. I discovered it, in fact, as it had been dictated up to these words: "The Father is only the Father, and the Son is not other than the Son, because, even when he is called the likeness of the Father, although it shows that there is no dissimilarity between them, nonetheless the Father is not alone if he has a likeness."[264] After this I repeated the words of scripture, *And God said, Let us make man to our image and likeness* (Gn 1:26), in order to consider and discuss them again. I had left the book incomplete at that point. What follows this I thought should be added when I was revising it; I did not complete it, though, and once this was added I left it incomplete. For, if I had completed it, I would at least have discussed all the works and words of God that pertain to the sixth day. I thought it would be superfluous to draw attention to the things in this book that dissatisfy me, or to defend things that were not well thought out and that could dissatisfy others, if not correctly understood. Instead, to be brief, I recommend that those twelve books be read which I composed long after as a bishop; let a judgment on this book be made on the basis of them.

And so this [book] begins in this way: "Our purpose is to discuss—not through assertions but by inquiry—the obscurities of the natural world, which we know were made by almighty God, their creator."

19 (18). TWO BOOKS
ON THE LORD'S SERMON ON THE MOUNT
(De Sermone Domini In Monte Libri Duo)[265]

1. During the same period I wrote two volumes on the Lord's Sermon on the Mount according to Matthew. In the first of them,

---

264. 16,60.
265. Probably written in 393.

apropos of what is written, *Blessed are the peacemakers, for they shall be called sons of God* (Mt 5:9), I said, "Wisdom belongs to peacemakers, in whom all things have already been set in order and there is no rebellious movement against reason, but everything submits to a person's spirit, just as he himself submits to God."[266] The way in which I spoke is truly problematic. For no one can make such progress in this life that the law fighting against the law of our mind[267] is utterly absent from our members, since, even if a person's spirit resisted it in such a way that it never slipped into giving assent to it, it [i.e., that law] would still continue to fight against it. What I said, then, that there would be no rebellious movement against reason, can be correctly understood with regard to those who are now acting on behalf of peace by overcoming the desires of the flesh, so that at some time that fullness of peace may be attained.

2. Then, in another passage, when I had repeated the same words of the gospel, *Blessed are the peacemakers, for they shall be called sons of God*, I added, "And these things can certainly be realized in this life,[268] as we believe that they were realized in the apostles."[269] This should not be understood in such a way that we would think that in the apostles, while they were living here, there was no movement of the flesh fighting against the spirit; rather, these things can be realized here to the same extent that we believe they were realized in the apostles—namely, in accordance with that measure of human perfection, which is as much perfection as can exist in this life. For it was not said that these things could be realized in this life because we believe that they were realized in the apostles, but what was said was "as we believe that they were realized in the apostles," so that they would be realized as they were realized in them—that is, to the degree of perfection that this life is capable of—and not as they are going to be real-

266. I,4,11.
267. See Rom 7:23.
268. The realization of "these things" refers to the realization of the promises associated with the first seven beatitudes, up to *Blessed are the peacemakers....*
269. I,4,12.

ized, thanks to that utter peace for which we hope, when it will be said, *Where, O death, is your strife?* (1 Cor 15:55)

3. In another passage I used the testimony, *For God does not give the Spirit according to measure* (Jn 3:34),[270] without having understood at the time that this is more accurately taken to refer to Christ himself. For, indeed, unless the Spirit were given to other men according to measure, Elisha would not have asked for the double of what Elijah had.[271]

Again, when I was explaining what was written, *Not one iota or the smallest part of a letter shall depart from the law until all things are accomplished* (Mt 5:18), I said, "This cannot be understood except as a forceful expression of perfection."[272] Here the question is appropriately raised as to whether this perfection can be understood in such a way that it is still true that no one who is now making use of the choice of the will lives here without sin. For by whom can the law be perfectly carried out, even to the smallest part of a letter, except by the one who accomplishes all the divine commandments? But among these same commandments there is also what we are commanded to say, *Forgive us our debts, as we forgive our debtors* (Mt 6:12), which is the prayer that the entire Church says until the end of the world. All the commandments are therefore considered to have been accomplished when whatever is not accomplished is pardoned.

4. What the Lord said, *Whoever fails to observe one of these least commandments and teaches thus* (Mt 5:19), and so forth, up to the passage where it says, *Unless your righteousness exceeds that of the scribes and Pharisees, you shall not enter into the kingdom of heaven* (Mt 5:20), I certainly explained much better and more suitably in other later sermons of mine,[273] which would take too long to repeat here. The thrust [of these words] leads to the conclusion that the righteousness of those who speak and do

270. I,6,17.
271. See 2 K 2:9.
272. I,8,20.
273. These sermons do not seem to have survived.

is greater than that of the scribes and Pharisees. The Lord himself says of the scribes and Pharisees in another passage, *For they speak and do not do* (Mt 23:3).

We also understood better afterwards[274] what is written, *The one who is angry at his brother* (Mt 5:22).[275] For the Greek codexes do not have *without cause*, as appears here,[276] although the sense is the same. For we said that one must see what it means to be angry at one's brother, because one who is not angry at his brother is not angry at his brother's sin. One who is not angry at his brother's sin, therefore, is angry without cause.

5. Again, I said, "This must be understood of father and mother and other blood relations, so that we hate in them what fell to the human race through being born and dying."[277] This sounds as though these relationships would not have existed if, without some antecedent sin of human nature, no one were going to die. This understanding I have already condemned previously.[278] For there certainly would have been families and relationships even if there had been no original sin; the human race would have increased and multiplied without death. And so the problem as to why the Lord commanded that enemies be loved[279] must be solved in another way, given that in another passage he commands that parents and children be hated. It is not solved as it is here but as we often solved it later[280]—that is, we should love our enemies in order to gain them for the kingdom of God and hate in those nearest us whatever obstacle there is to the kingdom of God.

6. Again, I certainly discussed here very carefully the precept forbidding the dismissal of one's wife except on account

---

274. See *The City of God* XXI,27.
275. I,9,22.25.
276. The text that Augustine used read *the one who is angry at his brother without cause*, which was known to, and rejected as inauthentic by, some other ancient Christian authors as well—namely, Origen, Apollinaris, Ps.-Athanasius and Jerome. See Amy M. Donaldson, *Explicit References to New Testament Variant Readings among Greek and Latin Church Fathers* (diss. Notre Dame, Ind. 2009) 348-353.
277. I,15,41. See Lk 14:26.
278. See *Revisions* I,10,2; 13,8.
279. See Mt 5:44; Lk 6:27.
280. See *The City of God* XXI,26.

of fornication.[281] But what the Lord wanted to be understood by the fornication on account of which he would permit a wife to be dismissed must repeatedly be thought through and investigated—whether that which is condemned is lewd behavior or that of which it is said, *You have destroyed everyone who fornicates away from you* (Ps 73:27), which certainly includes the previous one (for he who *takes the members of Christ and makes them members of a prostitute* [1 Cor 6:15] is also fornicating away from the Lord). I do not want the reader to think that, in regard to this matter, which is so important and so difficult to make a determination about, this discussion of ours should suffice. He should read other works as well, whether works of ours that were written later[282] or those of others that offer a more careful treatment. Otherwise, if he can, he himself should pursue with an especially vigilant and probing mind the things that could rightfully cause confusion here. Because not every sin is fornication and because God, who hears his holy ones when each day they say, *Forgive us our debts*, does not destroy every sinner (although *he destroys everyone who fornicates away from him*), the most obscure question is how this fornication should be understood and defined, and whether even on account of it one is permitted to dismiss one's wife. On the other hand, there is no question that it is permitted on account of what is perpetrated in lewd behavior. And when I said that this was permitted and not commanded, I did not heed another scripture that says, *He who takes an adulteress is foolish and wicked* (Prv 18:22). I certainly would not have said that that woman should be considered an adulteress, even after she heard from the Lord, *Nor do I condemn you; go, and from now on do not sin any more* (Jn 8:11), if she listened obediently to this.

7. In another passage touching on what John says, *I do not say that one should pray for this* (1 Jn 5:16), I defined a brother's sin unto death in this way: "I think that a brother's sin unto death ex-

281. I,16,43. See Mt 5:32.
282. See *Observations on the Heptateuch* II,71; Sermon 162.

ists when, after knowing God through the grace of our Lord Jesus Christ, he attacks the brotherhood and is agitated by torches of hatred against the very grace by which he was reconciled to God."[283] I did not actually affirm this, because I said that this was what I thought, but this should nonetheless have been added—"if he were to finish his life in this wicked perversity of mind"[284]—because a very bad person living in this life should certainly not be despaired of, nor is it imprudent to pray for a person who is not despaired of.

8. Again, in the second book I said, "No one will be allowed to be unaware of the kingdom of God, since his only-begotten Son will come from heaven not only in intelligible fashion but even visibly, as the Lordly Man, to judge the living and the dead."[285] But I do not see whether he who is *the mediator of God and men, the man Christ Jesus* (1 Tm 2:5), is appropriately referred to as a Lordly Man, although he is certainly the Lord. Who in his holy household cannot be called a lordly man?[286] And indeed, as for my saying this—I read it in some Catholic commentators on the divine scriptures. But wherever I said this, I wish that I had not said it.[287]

Again, what I said, "There is hardly anyone whose conscience hates God,"[288] I see should not have been said, for there are many of whom it is written, *The pride of those who hate you* (Ps 74:23).

9. There is another passage in which I said, "The Lord said, *Sufficient for the day is its own evil* (Mt 6:34), because need itself

---

283. I,22,73.
284. In other words Augustine's sentence would be modified along these lines: "I think that a brother's sin unto death exists when, after knowing God through the grace of our Lord Jesus Christ, he attacks the brotherhood and is agitated by torches of hatred against the very grace by which he was reconciled to God, and if he were to finish his life in this wicked perversity of mind."
285. II,6,20. See 2 Tm 4:1.
286. "Lordly Man": *homo dominicus*. The expression can also be rendered as "man of the Lord" or "the Lord's man," which are probably better translations for members of the "holy household"—namely, the Church. They do not make sense, however, in reference to Christ himself.
287. On this controversial term and its use in patristic literature see Alois Grillmeier, "Jesus Christ, the Kyriakos Anthropos," in *Theological Studies* 38 (1977) 275-293; idem, "*O kyriakos anthropos*: Eine Studie zu einer christologischen Bezeichnung der Väterzeit," in *Traditio* 33 (1977) 1-63.
288. II,14,48.

will require the taking of food. I think that this is called evil, because it is a punishment for us, since it is associated with that frailty which we merited by sinning."[289] Here I failed to recall the foods for the body that were also given to the first human beings in paradise before they merited the punishment of death by sinning. [290] For, in a body that was not yet spiritual but animal, they were immortal in such a way that, in this kind of immortality, they still made use of bodily foods.

Again, I said, "Which God has chosen for himself, *a glorious Church that has no spot or wrinkle*" (Eph 5:27).[291] I did not say this because now and in every regard it is already such, although there should be no doubt that it has been chosen for this, so that it may be like that when Christ, its life, appears,[292] for then it will also appear with him in the glory on account of which the Church has been called glorious.[293]

Again, apropos of what the Lord said, *Ask and you shall receive, seek and you shall find, knock and it shall be opened to you* (Mt 7:7), I thought that how these three things differ from one another should be painstakingly examined,[294] but all of them are much better reduced to a very urgent petition. This is clear, in fact, from when he concluded everything with the same word and said, *How much more will your Father who is in heaven give good things to those who ask him* (Mt 7:11), for he did not say "to those who ask and seek and knock."

This work begins in this way: "The sermon that the Lord gave."

---

289. II,17,56.
290. See Gn 1:29; 2:9.16.
291. II,19,66.
292. See Col 3:4.
293. See p. 41, n. 92.
294. II,21,71-73.

20 (19). A Psalm Against The Party Of Donatus
(Psalmus Contra Partem Donati)[295]

Wishing also to bring the issue of the Donatists[296] to the attention of the very simplest people and, in general, of the ignorant and unlearned, and to do so in a way that would be as easy for them to remember as possible, I made up a psalm that went through the Latin alphabet and that could be sung by them, but it only got as far as the letter V. Things of this sort are referred to as abecedarian. While it is true that I left out the final three [letters],[297] in place of them I added something at the end to serve as a sort of epilogue, as though Mother Church were speaking to them. The refrain as well, which is a response, and the introduction of the issue, which would nonetheless be sung, are not in the sequence of the letters; their sequence begins after the introduction. I did not want to do this in some other song-form lest the requirements of meter would force some words on me that were less well known to the general public.

This psalm begins in this way: "All you who rejoice over peace, now judge the truth." This is also its refrain.

21 (20). One Book In Answer To A Letter
Of The Heretic Donatus
(Contra Epistolam Donati Heretici Liber Unus)[298]

1. During the same period of my presbyterate I also wrote a book against a letter of Donatus, who was the second bishop of the party of Donatus at Carthage after Majorinus.[299] In this

---

295. Written between the end of 393 and the beginning of 394.

296. The Donatists were a sect within the Christian Church that arose in North Africa at the beginning of the fourth century and, in essence, claimed to be purer than the Catholic Church. While reflecting Catholic practice in many respects, Donatism rejected the validity of the Catholic sacraments. As this and subsequent entries in the *Revisions* show, Donatism was a preoccupation of Augustine's for well over a decade.

297. In Latin the letters of the alphabet after V are X, Y and Z; there is no W.

298. This work, which was lost after Augustine composed the *Revisions*, was probably written between 393 and 395.

299. Majorinus was bishop of Carthage from 308 or 312 until 314 and the founder of the sect that later came to be known as Donatism. Donatus, who succeeded him at Car-

letter he contends that it should not be believed that there is any baptism in Christ outside of his communion, which we contradict in this book.

In it I said of the apostle Peter in a certain passage that "the Church was founded upon him as upon a rock." This notion is also sung by many mouths in the verses of the most blessed Ambrose, when he says of the crowing cock, "As it crowed, he himself, the Church's rock, washed sin away."[300] But I know that later I very often explained[301] what was said by the Lord, *You are Peter, and upon this rock I will build my Church* (Mt 16:18), in such a way that it would be understood [as being built] upon him whom Peter confessed when he said, *You are the Christ, the Son of the living God* (Mt 16:16). Thus Peter, who was named after that rock, would signify the role of the Church that is built upon this rock and that received the keys of the kingdom of heaven.[302] For it was not said to him, "You are the rock," but rather, *You are Peter. But the rock was Christ* (1 Cor 10:4). This was the one whom Simon confessed (and he was called Peter), just as the whole Church confesses him. Let the reader choose, though, which of these two opinions is the more likely.[303]

2. In another passage I said, "God seeks the death of no one," which should be taken to mean that a person who has abandoned God has brought death upon himself, and he who does not return to God brings it upon himself, in accordance with what is written, *God did not make death* (Wis 1:13). But it is also no less true that *life and death is from the Lord God* (Sir 11:14)—namely, life is from its giver, death from its vindicator.

---

thage and was bishop until 347, was such an organizing genius and so charismatic a leader that the sect was soon called by his name. No theological writing of his has survived in its entirety, although he is occasionally cited by Augustine and others.
300. Ambrose, Hymn I,4.
301. See Sermon 76,1,1.
302. See Mt 16:19.
303. The first opinion is that Peter is the rock, the second that Christ is the rock. The Latin word for rock, *petra*, prompts Augustine's exegesis. The meaning of *rock* in Mt 16:18 was much discussed in early Christian exegesis. See J. Ludwig, *Die Primatsworte Mt 16:18-19 in der altkirchlichen Exegese* (Münster 1952).

3. Again, I said that Donatus, whose letter I was refuting, "asked the emperor to provide bishops from across the sea to judge between himself and Caecilian."[304] It is more likely that it was not he but another Donatus who did this—although of the same schism. The latter, however, was the bishop of the Donatists not at Carthage but at Casae Nigrae; yet he was the first to perpetrate the abominable schism at Carthage itself. Neither was it Donatus of Carthage who determined that Christians should be rebaptized, which I believed he had determined when I was responding to his letter. Neither did he delete from the Book of Ecclesiasticus words from the middle of a sentence that were pertinent to the matter, where it is written, *He who is baptized by a dead man and touches him again: of what value is his washing?* (Sir 34:25)[305] This man put it down as though it were written, *He who is baptized by a dead man: of what value is his washing?* But afterwards we learned that, even before there was a party of Donatus, there were many codexes (African ones, however) that did not have *and touches him again* in the middle. If I had known this at the time I would not have been so outspoken against him as a thief and violator of divine scripture.

This book begins in this way: "I had heard from you yourself, in your presence."

22 (21). ONE BOOK IN ANSWER TO ADIMANTUS, A DISCIPLE OF MANI

(Contra Adimantum Manichaei Discipulum Liber Unus)[306]

1. At the same time there fell into my hands some disputations of Adimantus, who had been a disciple of Mani. He wrote them against the law and the prophets in an attempt to show that

---

304. See *On Baptism* VI,34,65; *Answer to Cresconius* II,27,33. Caecilian was elected bishop of Carthage in 308 or 311, despite his great unpopularity. Majorinus was elected the following year in opposition to him. Caecilian was vindicated several times and lived until after 325, but he never seems to have enjoyed the affection of his people and clergy.
305. See Letter 108,2,6.
306. Written in 394.

the gospels and the apostolic writings were contrary to them.[307] I responded to him, then, by setting out his words and giving my response to them. I completed this work in one volume, and in it I responded to some questions not once but twice, because my first response had gotten lost and then was found when I had already responded again. In fact I resolved some of these same questions in my sermons to the people in church.[308] I have still not responded to others: some remained that were put aside on account of more urgent matters, and to that has been added an increasing forgetfulness as well.

2. In this I said, then, "For, in accordance with the marvelous and most orderly dispensation of the times, the people who accepted the Old Testament were, before the Lord's coming, held bound by certain shadows and figures of things, yet in them [i.e., in the people] there is such an announcement and proclamation of the New Testament that there are no divine precepts and promises, however lofty, which are found in the gospels and in the apostolic teaching that are missing from those ancient books."[309] But I should have added "almost," and I should have said that "there are *almost* no divine precepts and promises, however lofty, which are found in the gospels and in the apostolic teaching that are missing from those ancient books." For why is it that the Lord says in the Sermon on the Mount in the gospel, *You have heard that this was said to the men of old, but I say this to you* (Mt 5:21-22), if he himself commanded nothing more than was commanded in those ancient books? Moreover, among the things that were promised by the law given through Moses on Mount Sinai,[310] which is properly called the Old Testament, we do not read that the kingdom of heaven was promised to that people. The Apostle says that it [i.e., the Old Testament] was prefigured

307. Opposing the Old Testament and the New, to the advantage of the New, was typical of the Manicheans.
308. See Sermons 1; 50; 142; 153.
309. 3,4.
310. See Ex 19:3-4.

by Sarah's maid and her son, but the New was also symbolized there by Sarah herself and her own son.[311] If, then, it is symbols that are being discussed, everything is found prophesied there that Christ brought about or that we wait for him to bring about. Nevertheless, because there are certain precepts that are not figurative but literal, which are found not in the Old Testament but in the New, it would have been more cautious and moderate to say that there are "almost no" rather than "no" [precepts] in the latter that are not also in the former, although in the former there are those two precepts of love of God and neighbor[312] to which everything, whether of the law or of the prophets or of the gospels or of the apostles, is most correctly referred.

3. Again, when I said, "The term 'sons' is used in three ways in the holy scriptures,"[313] it was said with insufficient thought, for there is no doubt that we omitted certain other ways. For instance, *son of Gehenna* (Mt 23:15) is said, and also *adoptive son* (Rom 8:15; Gal 4:5), and these are certainly not said according to nature or according to teaching or according to imitation. We gave examples of these three ways as though they were the only ones: according to nature, as the Jews are *sons of Abraham* (Jn 8:37); according to teaching, as the Apostle calls his sons those whom he has taught the gospel;[314] according to imitation, as we are sons of Abraham, whose faith we imitate.[315]

When I said, "When it puts on incorruption and immortality[316] it will no longer be flesh and blood,"[317] it was in reference to fleshly corruption that it was said that it will not be flesh, not in reference to its substance, in accordance with which the Lord's body was called flesh even after the resurrection.[318]

311. See Gal 4:22-31.
312. See Lv 19:18; Dt 6:5; and also Mt 22:37-40 par.
313. 5,1.
314. See 1 Cor 4:14-15.
315. See Gal 3:7.
316. See 1 Cor 15:54.
317. 12,5.
318. See Lk 24:39.

4. In another passage I said, "Unless someone changes his will he cannot accomplish the good that he [i.e., Christ] teaches in another passage has been placed in our power, when he says, *Either make the tree good and its fruit good, or make the tree bad and its fruit bad* (Mt 12:33)."[319] This is not against the grace of God, which we proclaim. It is indeed in a person's power to change his will for the better, but there is no such power unless it is given by God, of whom it is said, *He gave them power to become sons of God* (Jn 1:12). For, since it is in our power to do what we will, there is nothing that is so much in our power as the will itself, but *the will is made ready by the Lord* (Prv 8:35 LXX). It is in that way, then, that he gives the power. That is also how what I said afterwards should be understood, "It is in our power to merit either to be grafted in by God's goodness or to be cut off by his severity,"[320] because it is not in our power unless it follows our will; when it is made ready by the Lord it is strong and powerful and easily accomplishes even a work of piety that was difficult and impossible.

This book begins in this way: "Concerning what is written: *In the beginning God made heaven and earth* (Gn 1:1)."

23 (22). A Commentary On Some Statements In The Apostle's Epistle To The Romans
(Expositio Quarumdam Propositionum Ex Epistola Apostoli Ad Romanos)[321]

1. While I was still a presbyter, it happened that the Apostle's Epistle to the Romans was read among us who were together at Carthage, and I was asked some things by the brothers. When I responded to them as well as I could, they wanted what I said to be written down rather than be spoken without being recorded. When I acceded to them, one book was added to my previous works.

---

319. 26,1.
320. 27,1.
321. Written in 394.

In that book I said, "When he [i.e., Paul] says, *We know that the law is spiritual, but I am fleshly* (Rom 7:14), he shows clearly that the law cannot be fulfilled except by spiritual persons, such as God's grace makes."[322] This I was unwilling to accept as representing the Apostle, who was already spiritual, but as representing man, set under the law and not yet under grace.[323] For that was how I first understood these words, which later, after having read some expositors of divine scripture whose authority swayed me,[324] I considered more carefully, and I saw that what he said, *We know that the law is spiritual, but I am fleshly*, could also be applied to the Apostle himself. I have carefully pointed this out, as well as I could, in the books that I have recently written against the Pelagians.[325]

In this book this was also said: *But I am fleshly*, and so forth, up to the passage where it says, *Wretched man that I am, who will free me from the body of this death? The grace of God through Jesus Christ our Lord.* (Rom 7:24-25) I said that this was a description of a man still set under the law and not yet under grace, who wishes to do what is good but, overcome by the concupiscence of the flesh, does what is evil. Nothing frees him from the domination of this concupiscence but *the grace of God through Jesus Christ our Lord* (Rom 7:25). By the gift of the Holy Spirit, through whom *charity has been poured forth in our hearts* (Rom 5:5), it overcomes the concupiscences of the flesh, so that we do not yield to them so as to do what is evil but so that, instead, we do what is good. That is how at this moment the Pelagian heresy is overthrown, which wants the charity whereby we live good and holy lives to come not from God to us but from ourselves. But, in the books that we published against them,[326] we showed that those words are better applied to the spiritual man who is already set under grace. This is so because

---

322. 41.
323. See Rom 1:11; 6:14-15.
324. See, e.g., Ambrose, *On Penitence* I,3,13.
325. See *The Grace of Christ* 43; *Answer to the Two Letters of the Pelagians* I,17-25; *Unfinished Work in answer to Julian* I,99; Sermon 154; *Commentary on the Epistle to the Galatians* 5; *The City of God* XXII,21; and also *Revisions* I,26,2, question 66.
326. See *The Grace of Christ* 39.43-44; *Answer to the Two Letters of the Pelagians* I,10,17; *The Perfection of Human Righteousness* 11,28.

of the body of the flesh, which is not yet spiritual but will be such in the resurrection of the dead, and also because of the concupiscence of the flesh, with which the saints are in conflict. Although they do not yield to it for the purpose of evil, nonetheless in this life they are not spared its disturbances, which they resist as they fight against them, but they will not have them in that [life] where *death will be swallowed up in victory* (1 Cor 15:54). And because of this concupiscence and its disturbances, which are resisted in such a way that they nonetheless exist in us, each saint who is already set under grace can say all those things that I have said here were the words of the man who is not yet set under grace but under the law. It would be too long to show this here, and where I have shown it has been mentioned.

2. Again, I was discussing what it was that God chose in the one who was not yet born, whom he said that the older would serve, and what he rejected in him who was older and similarly not yet born. (Although it was long afterwards that the prophetic testimony was offered,[327] this is what is said about them in that respect: *I loved Jacob, but I hated Esau* [Rom 9:13].) In this regard I reasoned as follows: "God, then, did not choose the works—which he himself was going to bestow—of either one of them in his foreknowledge, but in his foreknowledge he chose faith, in that way choosing the very one who he foreknew was going to believe in him, to whom he would give the Holy Spirit, so that by performing good works he would also attain to eternal life."[328] I had not yet carefully examined, nor up to that point had I found, what sort of thing grace's choosing might be, of which the same Apostle says, *A remnant was saved through grace's choosing* (Rom 11:15). It is not grace, to be sure, if any merits precede it, so that what is given is paid back on account of merits, not in accordance with grace but as something owed, rather than as a gift.

---

327. See Mal 1:2-3. This prophetic testimony was offered long afterwards because the original incident is recorded toward the beginning of the Old Testament, in Gn 27:1-45. Mal is the final prophetic book in the Old Testament.
328. 60.

Then I said immediately after that, "For the same Apostle says, *The same God who works all in all* (1 Cor 12:6), but nowhere is it said, 'God believes all in all,' " and then I added, "What we believe, therefore, is ours, but the good that we do is his who gives the Holy Spirit to those who believe."[329] I would certainly not have said this if I knew then that even faith itself is among God's gifts that are given *in the same Spirit* (1 Cor 12:9). Each[330] is ours, then, because of the choice of the will, and yet each is given by the Spirit of faith and charity. For not charity alone, but, as it is written, *Charity with faith is from God the Father and our Lord Jesus Christ* (Eph 6:23).

3. And what I said shortly afterwards is certainly true: "For believing and willing are ours, but it is his to give to those who believe and who will the ability to do good through the Holy Spirit, by whom *charity is poured forth in our hearts*."[331] But by this same rule, however, both are his, because it is he who readies the will,[332] and both are ours, because nothing is done unless we will it.

And for the same reason what I also said later is entirely true: "We are unable to will unless we are called, and, although we will after a call, our willing and our running are insufficient unless God supplies the strength to those who run and leads them where he is calling them," after which I added, "It is clear, then, that *it is not because of the one who wills nor because of the one who runs but because of God who is merciful* (Rom 9:16) that we do what is good."[333] But I discussed inadequately the calling itself, which comes about in accordance with God's plan. For it does not apply to all who are called but only to those who have been chosen. And so what I said shortly afterwards I said most truly: "Just as in those whom God chooses it is not works but faith that initiates merit, so that it is by God's gift that they do what is good, so in those whom he condemns it is lack of faith and wickedness that initiate

---

329. Ibid.
330. I.e., faith and good works, or faith and charity.
331. 61.
332. See Prv 8:35 LXX.
333. 62.

the merit of punishment, so that by way of punishment itself they also do what is bad."[334] But I neither thought that the merit of faith was itself a gift of God, nor did I say that it needed to be examined.

4. And in another passage I said, "For him to whom he is merciful he causes to do what is good, and him whom he hardens he abandons to do what is bad. But that mercy is also bestowed by reason of the antecedent merit of faith, and that hardening by antecedent wickedness."[335] That is certainly true. Yet it still had to be examined whether the merit of faith also comes from God's mercy[336]—that is, whether that mercy is brought about in a person because he is faithful or whether it has been brought about so that he might be faithful. We read that the Apostle says, *I received mercy so that I might be faithful* (1 Cor 7:25). He did not say, "Because I was faithful." To be sure, then, it is given to a faithful person, but it was also given so that he might be faithful. And so I said most correctly in another passage in the same book, "Because, if we are called not by works but by God's mercy so that we may believe, and if he makes it possible for us who believe to do what is good, this mercy should not be begrudged to the pagans."[337] Nonetheless I did not discuss carefully the call whereby God's plan is carried out.

This book begins in this way: "These are the ideas in the Epistle of the apostle Paul to the Romans."

24 (23). A COMMENTARY ON THE EPISTLE TO THE GALATIANS, IN ONE BOOK
(Expositio Epistolae Ad Galatas Liber Unus)[338]

1. After this book I commented on the same Apostle's Epistle to the Galatians not piecemeal—that is, omitting some things—

---

334. Ibid.
335. Ibid.
336. Another reading has "whether the merit of faith precedes God's mercy," which is the contrary but not opposed to Augustine's argument.
337. 64.
338. Written during the years 394 and 395.

but continuously and in its entirety. I completed it, however, within a single volume.

In it this was said: "The first apostles, who were truthful, were sent not by men but by God through a man, through Jesus Christ, who was still mortal. The last Apostle too, who was truthful, was sent through Jesus Christ, now fully God, after his resurrection."[339] "Now fully God" was said because of the immortality that he began to possess after the resurrection, not because of the ever-immortal divinity from which he never withdrew, in which he was fully God even when he was still going to die. What follows makes this meaning clear, for I added and said, "First the other apostles are [sent] through Christ, still partly a man—that is, mortal. Last the Apostle Paul is [sent] through Christ, now fully God—that is, immortal in every respect."[340] I said this in explaining what the Apostle said, *Not by men nor through a man, but through Jesus Christ and God the Father* (Gal 1:1), as though Jesus Christ were no longer a man. For it follows, *Who raised him from the dead* (Gal 1:1), which makes it obvious why he said *nor through a man*. Accordingly it is on account of his immortality that Christ, God, is now no longer man, while on account of the substance of human nature, in which he ascended into heaven, he is now also *the mediator of God and men, the man Christ Jesus* (1 Tm 2:5), because he will come back in the same way as they saw him who saw him going into heaven.[341]

2. Again, what I said, "It is God's grace by which our sins are forgiven so that we *may* be reconciled to God, but it is peace by which we *are* reconciled to God,"[342] should be understood in such a way that we still also recognize that both [grace and peace] belong to God's general grace, just as in the people of God Israel on the one hand and Judah on the other are specific entities, and yet both are Israel in a general way.

---

339. 2,3.
340. 2,4.
341. See Acts 1:11.
342. 3.

Again, when I was commenting on *Why then? The law was set forth because of transgression* (Gal 3:19), I thought that a separation should be made in such a way that there was a question, *Why then?* followed by a response, *The law was set forth because of transgression.*[343] This is, to be sure, not inconsistent with the truth, but it seems to me that the separation would be better if this were the question: *Why then is there the law?* And then there would be the response: *It was set forth because of transgression.*[344]

I also said, "He adds, then, in the most proper order, *If you are led by the Spirit, you are no longer under the law* (Gal 5:18), so that we may understand that they are under the law whose spirit so lusts against the flesh that they do not do what they will—that is, that they do not maintain themselves unconquered in the charity of righteousness—but are conquered by their flesh, which lusts against them."[345] This is how I understood what was said, *The flesh lusts against the spirit, and the spirit against the flesh, for they are mutually opposed, so that you do not do the things that you will* (Gal 5:17), when I thought that it pertained to those who were under the law and not yet under grace. For I had still not understood that these words also apply to those who are under grace, and not under the law, because they themselves also have concupiscences of the flesh, against which they lust in spirit, although they do not consent to them; yet, if that were possible, they would will not to have any. And they do not do whatever they will because they will to be without them but are unable to be. For they will not have them when they do not have corruptible flesh.

This book begins in this way: "This is the reason why the Apostle writes to the Galatians."

---

343. 24.
344. The Latin text of Gal 3:19 allows for both possibilities. Augustine also opts for the latter reading in Letter 82,20.
345. 47.

25 (24). An Unfinished Commentary On The Epistle To The Romans, In One Book
(Epistolae Ad Romanos Inchoata Expositio Liber Unus)[346]

I also undertook a commentary on the Epistle to the Romans, as I did on the Epistle to the Galatians. If it were complete, there would be many books in this work. I finished one of them, which was devoted exclusively to the salutation itself—namely, from the beginning until where it says, *Grace to you and peace from God our Father and the Lord Jesus Christ* (Rom 1:7). It happened that we stopped when we wanted to resolve a very difficult question that was raised in a sermon of ours[347] about the sin against the Holy Spirit, *which is forgiven neither in this world nor in the one to come* (Mt 12:32). But then I ceased adding other volumes that would have commented on the entire epistle, since I was discouraged by the vastness and difficulty of the project, and I let myself turn to other things that were easier. That is how it happened that I left the first book that I had composed as the only one, which I wanted to be entitled *An Unfinished Commentary on the Epistle to the Romans.*

I said that there was "grace in the forgiveness of sins but peace in reconciliation with God,"[348] and wherever I said this it should not be understood as though this very peace and reconciliation do not belong to general grace, but what they signify in a specific way is the remission of sins under the name of grace, just as we speak of the law in both a specific way, in accordance with the phrase *the law and the prophets* (Mt 22:40; Rom 3:21), and in a general way, so that the prophets are included in it.

This book begins in this way: "In the epistle that the apostle Paul wrote to the Romans."

---

346. Written in 394.
347. Sermon 71.
348. 23.

26 (25). One Book Containing
a Miscellany Of Eighty-Three Questions
(De Diversis Quaestionibus Octoginta Tribus
Liber Unus)[349]

1. Among the things that we have written there is also a certain lengthy work, which is nonetheless counted as a single book, entitled *A Miscellany of Eighty-three Questions.* They were scattered on numerous pieces of paper because, from the time when I was first converted, after we came to Africa, they were dictated by me in the same random order as the brothers asked me questions, when they saw that I had time to spare. When I was already a bishop I ordered that they be collected and made into a single book, which is in numbered sections, so that whoever wants to read something may find it easily.

2. Of these questions the first is whether the soul exists of itself. The second is on free choice.

The third asks whether it is by God's causality that humankind is evil.

The fourth asks why humankind is evil.

The fifth asks whether an irrational animal can be happy.

The sixth is on evil.

The seventh is on what should properly be called the soul in an ensouled being.

The eighth asks whether the soul is moved by itself.

The ninth asks whether truth can be grasped by the body's senses. In it I said, "Everything that a bodily sense attains, which is also referred to as sensible, is subject to continual temporal change." Without a doubt this is certainly not true of the incorruptible bodies of the resurrection. But now no bodily sense of ours attains them unless perhaps something of the sort is divinely revealed.

---

349. Compiled from questions raised between 388 and 395, and composed in 395. From 388 to 391 Augustine lived in a community of like-minded religious men at Thagaste, and from 391 on he lived in another such community in Hippo. It was the members of those communities who posed the questions to which Augustine responds in this work.

The tenth asks whether the body is from God.

The eleventh asks why Christ was born of a woman.

The twelfth, which is entitled "The words of a certain wise man," is not mine, but it was through me that it became known to some of the brothers, who were then gathering my material very carefully. They liked it and wanted to place it among our writings. It comes from the work *On Purifying the Mind in order to See God* by a certain Fonteius of Carthage, which was in fact written when he was a pagan, although he died a baptized Christian.[350]

The thirteenth asks by what evidence it is clear that human beings are superior to beasts.

The fourteenth is on the fact that the body of our Lord Jesus Christ was not a phantom.

The fifteenth is on the intellect.

The sixteenth is on the Son of God.

The seventeenth is on God's knowledge.

The eighteenth is on the Trinity.

The nineteenth is on God and creation.

The twentieth is on God's place.

The twenty-first asks whether God is not the creator of evil. There it must be seen if what I said, "The creator of all things that exist is not the creator of evil, because to the extent that they exist they are good," might be misunderstood and give rise to the thought that the punishment of the wicked, which is indeed an evil to those who are punished by them, do not come from him. But I said this in the same way that it is said, *God did not make death* (Wis 1:13), although elsewhere it is written, *Death and life is from the Lord God* (Sir 11:14). The punishment of the wicked, then, which is from God, is certainly an evil to the wicked, but it is among God's good works, because it is just that the wicked be punished, and everything that is just is good indeed.

The twenty-second is on the fact that God is not subject to necessity.

---

350. This is all that is known of Fonteius, and what Augustine quotes in his *Miscellany* is all that survives of his writing.

The twenty-third is on the Father and the Son, where I said, "He himself begot the wisdom by which he is called wise." Afterwards, however, we dealt better with this question in the book on the Trinity.[351]

The twenty-fourth asks whether both committing sin and acting uprightly fall under the will's free choice. That this is the case is entirely true, but it is by the grace of God that one is free to act uprightly.

The twenty-fifth is on the cross of Christ.

The twenty-sixth is on the difference of sins.

The twenty-seventh is on providence.

The twenty-eighth is on why God willed to make the world.

The twenty-ninth asks whether anything is above or below in the universe.

The thirtieth asks whether everything has been created for the use of man.

The thirty-first is not mine either but Cicero's.[352] Because it too became known to the brothers through me, however, they placed it among the writings that they were collecting, wishing to know how the soul's virtues were differentiated and defined by him.

The thirty-second asks whether one person understands something better than another person, and whether the understanding of that thing can thus proceed to infinity.

The thirty-third is on fear.

The thirty-fourth asks whether nothing else should be loved than to lack fear.

The thirty-fifth is on what should be loved. I do not completely concur with what I said there: "That must be loved to possess which is nothing but to know."[353] For it was not that they did not possess God to whom it was said, *Do you not know that you are the temple of God and that the Spirit of God dwells in you?* (1 Cor 3:16) Yet they did not know him, or did not know him as he should

351. See *The Trinity* VI,2,3.
352. See Cicero, *De inventione* II,53,159-160.
353. 35,1.

have been known. Again, when I said, "No one, then, knows a happy life while being wretched,"[354] I said "knows" in terms of how it should be known. For who, among those who use their reason in this regard, is completely ignorant of it, since they know that they will to be happy?

The thirty-sixth is on fostering charity, where I said, "When God and the soul are loved, it is properly called charity, and it is it is most refined and most perfect, if nothing else is loved."[355] If this is true, why does the Apostle say, *No one ever hates his own flesh* (Eph 5:29), thus teaching that wives should be loved?[356] And that is why it was said, "It is properly called charity," because of course the flesh is loved, yet not properly but on account of the soul, to which it is subject for use. For even if it seems to be loved for its own sake, when we do not want it to be deformed, its beauty is to be referred to something else—namely, to that from which all beautiful things come.

The thirty-seventh is on him who has always been born.

The thirty-eighth is on the conformation of the soul.

The thirty-ninth is on foods.

The fortieth asks where the different wills of human beings come from, since souls have one nature.

The forty-first asks why, since God made all things, he did not make them in equal fashion.

The forty-second asks how the Lord Jesus Christ, who is the wisdom of God,[357] was both in his mother's womb and in heaven.

The forty-third asks why the Son of God appeared in a man and the Holy Spirit in a dove.[358]

The forty-fourth asks why the Lord Jesus Christ came after such a long time. When we were discussing the ages of the human race as if they were those of an individual person, I said, "It was not opportune for the Teacher, by whose imitation it [i.e., the hu-

354. Ibid.
355. 36,1.
356. See Eph 5:25.28.
357. See 1 Cor 1:24.
358. See Mt 3:16 par.

man race] would be formed for a most excellent manner of life, to come from heaven except during the period of its youth." And I added, "In this respect what the Apostle says is apropos—that under the law we were like children under a guardian's tutelage."[359] But it could be confusing that we said elsewhere that Christ came in the sixth age of the human race, in the old age of the old person, so to speak.[360] In the one place, then, what was said of youth refers to the vigor and fervor of faith *that works through love* (Gal 5:6), whereas in the other what was said of old age refers to the enumeration of the ages. For both can be understood of the whole of humankind, which cannot be the case in regard to the periods of life of individuals. Thus both youth and old age cannot co-exist in a body, but they can in a soul—the former through vivacity and the latter through gravity.

The forty-fifth is against mathematicians.[361]

The forty-sixth is on ideas.

The forty-seventh asks whether we may ever be able to see our thoughts. There I said, "It must be believed that angelic bodies, such as we hope to possess, are very light and ethereal." If this is understood to preclude the members that we now have or to preclude the substance of the flesh, albeit incorruptible, it is erroneous. This question on seeing our thoughts was treated much better in the work entitled *The City of God*.[362]

The forty-eighth is on believable things.

The forty-ninth asks why the children of Israel sacrificed oblations of cattle in visible fashion.

The fiftieth is on the equality of the Son.

The fifty-first is on man as made to the image and likeness of God. There I said, "Without life one may not correctly be called a man."[363] Is a man's corpse not also referred to as a man? Hence I

---

359. See Gal 3:23-24.
360. See, e.g., *On Genesis against the Manicheans* I,23,40.
361. Mathematician was a common term for astrologer.
362. See *The City of God* XXII,29.
363. 51,3.

should at least have said that it is not *properly* called such instead of saying that it is not *correctly* called such. [364] I also said, "Neither is this distinction useless—that the image and likeness of God is one thing, and being *in* the image and likeness of God, as we understand that man was made, is another."[365] This must not be understood as though man is not called the image of God, since the Apostle says, *A man*[366] *should certainly not cover his head, because he is the image and the glory of God* (1 Cor 11:7). But he is also said to be *in* the image of God, which is not the case with the Only-Begotten, who is only the image and not *in* the image.

The fifty-second is on what is said: *I regret having made man* (Gn 6:7).

The fifty-third is on the gold and silver that the Israelites took from the Egyptians.[367]

The fifty-fourth is on what is written: *But it is good for me to cling to God* (Ps 73:28). What I said there, "But that which is better than every soul we call God," ought rather to have been phrased "better than every created spirit."

The fifty-fifth is on what is written: *There are sixty queens and eighty concubines, and the young maidens are numberless* (Sg 6:8).

The fifty-sixth is on the forty-six years of the building of the Temple.[368]

The fifty-seventh is on the one hundred and fifty-three fish.[369]

The fifty-eighth is on John the Baptist.

The fifty-ninth is on the ten virgins.[370]

The sixtieth is on the words: *But of the day and the hour no one knows, neither the angels of heaven nor the Son of Man but only the Father* (Mt 24:36).

---

364. "Properly...correctly": *proprie...recte.*
365. 51,4.
366. Here "man" is *vir*; elsewhere in this section it is *homo.*
367. See Ex 3:22; 11:2; 12:35-36.
368. See Jn 2:20.
369. See Jn 21:6-11.
370. See Mt 25:1-13.

The sixty-first is on what is written in the gospel, that on the mountain the Lord fed the crowds with five loaves.[371] There I said, "The two fish seem to signify two offices—namely, kingship and priesthood—to which that most holy anointing also belonged."[372] "Especially belonged" should have been said here instead, because we sometimes read that the prophets were anointed.[373] I also said, "Luke, who hinted at Christ's priesthood when he ascended after the abolition of our sins, goes back to David through Nathan, because Nathan was the prophet who was sent at whose reproach David by his repentance obtained the abolition of his sin."[374] This should not be understood as though it were Nathan the prophet who was David's son, because it was not said here that he himself had been sent as a prophet but that "Nathan was the prophet who was sent." Thus the mystery would apply not to the same man but to the same name.[375]

The sixty-second is on what is written in the gospel, that *Jesus baptized more than John, although it was not he himself who baptized but his disciples* (Jn 4:1-2). There I said, "But that thief to whom it was said, *Amen, I say to you, today you will be with me in paradise* (Lk 23:43), who had not received baptism." In fact we discovered that other teachers of the holy Church had also said this in their writings before we did.[376] But I do not know by what proof it can be adequately demonstrated that that thief was not baptized. This matter has been given careful treatment in some of our later works, especially in that which we addressed to Vincent Victor on the origin of the soul.[377]

The sixty-third is on the Word.

The sixty-fourth is on the Samaritan woman.[378]

371. See Jn 6:3-13.
372. 61,2.
373. See, e.g., 1 K 19:16.
374. 61,2.
375. See also *Revisions* II,16, where the same issue is brought up.
376. See Cyprian, Letter 73,22.
377. See *The Soul and its Origin* I,9,11; III,9,12. Augustine corrects himself as well in *Revisions* II,18; 55,3.
378. See Jn 4:5-29.

The sixty-fifth is on the resurrection of Lazarus.[379]

The sixty-sixth is on what is written, *Are you unaware, brothers (for I speak to those who know the law), that a person is subject to the law for as long as he lives?* (Rom 7:1) up until the passage where it is written: *He will also give life to your mortal bodies through his Spirit dwelling in you* (Rom 8:11). What the Apostle said there, *We know that the law is spiritual, but I am fleshly* (Rom 7:14), I tried to explain by saying, "That is, since I have not yet been freed by spiritual grace I yield to the flesh."[380] This should not be understood as though a spiritual person already living under grace could not also say this, as well as the rest, in reference to himself, up until the passage where it is said, *Wretched man that I am, who will free me from the body of this death?* (Rom 7:24) This I learned later, as I have already previously acknowledged.[381] Again, explaining what the Apostle said, *The body indeed is dead on account of sin* (Rom 8:10), I said, "The body is said to be dead for as long as it disturbs the soul by its need for temporal things."[382] But later it seemed to me more accurate that the body is referred to as dead because it is now under the necessity of dying, which was not the case before sin.

The sixty-seventh is on what is written, *For I think that the sufferings of this time are insignificant in comparison to the glory that is to come that will be revealed in us* (Rom 8:18), up until what is said: *For by hope we have been saved* (Rom 8:24). When I was explaining the words, *And creation itself as well shall be freed from slavery to destruction* (Rom 8:21), I said, "*And creation itself*—that is, man himself, when after the mark of the image was lost because of sin, creation alone remained."[383] This should not be understood as though man lost in his entirety the image of God that he possessed. For, if it had not lost anything at all, the condition would not have existed on account of which it was said,

---

379. See Jn 11:17-44.
380. 66,5.
381. See *Revisions* I,23,2.
382. 66,6.
383. 67,4. The Latin for both "creation" and "creature" is *creatura*.

Be reformed in the newness of your mind (Rom 12:2), and, *We are being transformed into the same image* (2 Cor 3:18). But if, on the other hand, all of it were lost, nothing would have remained so that it could be said, *Although man walks in an image, yet he is disturbed in vain* (Ps 39:6). I also said, "The highest angels live spiritually but the lowest live in conformity with the animals."[384] This was said more rashly of the lowest than can be demonstrated either by the holy scriptures or by the facts themselves because, even if it can perhaps be demonstrated, it can be done only with great difficulty.

The sixty-eighth is on what is written: *O man, who are you that you talk back to God?* (Rom 9:20) There I said, "Because even if someone with lighter sins or even with any number of more serious ones has nonetheless, in his great groaning and the sorrow of his repentance, been accorded the mercy of God, it is not the doing of him who would perish if he were abandoned but the doing of a merciful God who comes to the aid of his entreaties and sorrow. For, if God is not merciful, it is not enough to will something, but God, who calls us to peace, is only merciful if the willing is already present."[385] This applies to the period after repentance. For, if God's mercy does not also precede the willing, the will would not be made ready by the Lord.[386] The calling itself, which also precedes faith, is part of that mercy. Treating of this a little later I said, "But this calling, which is at work at appropriate times whether in individual persons or in nations and in the human race itself, is of a lofty and profound ordering. Whence these words apply: *In the womb I sanctified you* (Jer 1:5), and, 'When you were in your father's loins I saw you,' and, *I loved Jacob, but I hated Esau* (Rom 9:13), and so forth. But how the words "When you were in your father's loins I saw you" struck me as scriptural I do not know.[387]

384. 67,5.
385. 68,5.
386. See Prv 8:35 LXX.
387. The words in question may be a rephrasing of Heb 7:10.

The sixty-ninth is on what is written: *Then the Son himself will be subjected to the one who has subjected everything to him* (1 Cor 15:28).

The seventieth is on what the Apostle says: *Death has been swallowed up in victory. Where, O death, is your struggle? Where, O death, is your sting? The sting of death is sin, but the strength of sin is the law.* (1 Cor 15:54-56)

The seventy-first is on what is written: *Bear one another's burdens, and thus you will fulfill the law of Christ* (Gal 6:2).

The seventy-second is on the eternal times.

The seventy-third is on what is written: *And found in form as a man* (Phil 2:7).

The seventy-fourth is on what is written in Paul's Epistle to the Colossians: *In whom we have redemption, the remission of sins, who is the image of the invisible God* (Col 1:14-15).

The seventy-fifth is on God's inheritance.

The seventy-sixth is on what the apostle James says: *Do you wish to know, O foolish person, that faith without works is useless?* (Jas 2:20)

The seventy-seventh asks whether fear is a sin.

The seventy-eighth is on the beauty of images.

The seventy-ninth asks why Pharaoh's magicians performed certain miracles as Moses, the servant of God did.[388]

The eightieth is against the Apollinarians.[389]

The eighty-first is on quadragesima and quinquagesima.[390]

The eighty-second is on what is written: *Whom the Lord loves he corrects; he scourges every son whom he receives* (Heb 12:16).

The eighty-third, on marriage, is on what the Lord says: *If anyone renounces his wife, except because of fornication* (Mt 5:32).

This work begins in this way: "Whether the soul exists of itself."

388. See Ex 7-8.
389. Apollinarianism took its name from Apollinarius, bishop of Laodicea, who lived from c. 310 to c. 390. The Apollinarians claimed that Christ did not have a human mind or soul and that the Word substituted for them.
390. I.e., periods of forty days and fifty days in the church calendar, now known as Lent and the Easter Season.

27 (26). ONE BOOK ON LYING
(De Mendacio Liber Unus)[391]

Again, I wrote a book on lying, which, even though it is somewhat difficult to understand, nonetheless provides a useful exercise of one's mental prowess and intelligence, and it is still more helpful towards developing a love of truthful speech in one's moral life. I had decided that it too be removed from my works[392] because it seemed to me to be obscure and complicated and altogether troublesome, which is why I had not published it. Then, when I afterwards wrote another [book] entitled *Against Lying*, I made an even firmer decision and prescribed that it be destroyed, but this was not carried out. And so, since I discovered that it was intact, I decided that, after being reviewed, it should remain in this revision of my works, especially because there are some important things in it that are not in that other one. That one's title is *Against Lying* while this one's is *On Lying* because in the former there is an open attack on lying throughout it, whereas a large part of the latter is given over to a discussion of the question; yet each is directed to the same end.

This book begins in this way: "Lying is a matter of great concern."

---

391. Written during the period 394-395 but not published until after the *Revisions* were composed.
392. I.e., like the *Unfinished Literal Commentary on Genesis*. See *Revisions* I,18.

Second Book

1 (28). Two Books For Simplician
(Ad Simplicianum Libri Duo)[1]

1. The first two books that I worked on as a bishop are addressed to Simplician, bishop of the church of Milan, who succeeded the most blessed Ambrose,[2] on a miscellany of questions. Two of them I took from the epistle of the apostle Paul to the Romans and put in the first book.

The first of these is on what is written, *What, then, shall we say? That the law is sin? By no means!* (Rom 7:7) up to the point where it says, *Who will free me from the body of this death? The grace of God through Jesus Christ our Lord.* (Rom 7:24-25) In it I explained those words of the Apostle—*The law is spiritual, but I am fleshly* (Rom 7:14), and so forth, by which the flesh is shown to struggle against the spirit—in such a way as though it described man *still set under the law* and *not yet under grace* (Rom 6:14). For it was not until long afterwards that I realized that those words can as well (and this is more likely) pertain to a spiritual person.

The second question in this book is from the passage where it says, *But in addition to her,[3] there is also Rebecca, who from a single act of intercourse conceived from our father Isaac* (Rom 9:10), up to the point where it says, *Unless the Lord of hosts had left us offspring, we would have become like Sodom, and we would have been like Gomorrah* (Rom 9:29). In answering this question I in fact strove on behalf of the free choice of the human will, but God's grace conquered, and otherwise I would have been unable to arrive at understanding what the Apostle said with the most evident truthfulness, *For who sets you apart? What do you possess that you have not received? But, if you have received,*

---

1. Written during the period 396-398. Simplician was bishop of Milan from 397 to 400 or 401.
2. Ambrose was bishop of Milan from 374 to 397.
3. I.e., Sarah.

why do you boast as though you had not received? (1 Cor 4:7) The martyr Cyprian also, wishing to demonstrate this, summed it all up with this very title when he said, "No one must boast of anything since nothing is ours."[4]

2. Other questions are treated in the second book and answered in accordance with whatever ability we had. They all concern the so-called Books of Kingdoms.[5]

The first of these is on what is written, *And the spirit of the Lord came over Saul* (1 S 10:10), inasmuch as it is said elsewhere, *And there was an evil spirit of the Lord in Saul* (1 S 16:14). In explaining this I said, "Although it is in a person's power to will something, nonetheless it is not in his power to be able to do it."[6] I said this because we do not say that something is in our power unless what we will happens, where the first and most important thing is the willing itself. Without any lapse of time whatsoever the will itself is present when we will. But we also receive the power from on high for living a good life when our will is made ready by the Lord.[7]

The second question asks how it was said, *I regret having made Saul king* (1 S 15:11).

The third asks whether the unclean spirit that was in the necromancer was able to bring it about that Samuel was seen by Saul and spoke with him.[8]

The fourth is on what is written: *King David went up and sat before the Lord* (2 S 7:18).

The fifth is on what Elijah said: *O Lord, witness of this widow with whom I am living in her home, you have done wrong by killing her son* (1 K 17:20).

This work begins in this way: "The clearly most welcome and delightful."

4. Cyprian, *Testimonies* III,4. A small collection of scriptural texts, including 1 Cor 4:7, is collected under this title. On Cyprian see p. 28, n. 18.
5. What Augustine knew as the four Books of Kingdoms are now referred to as two Books of Samuel and two Books of Kings.
6. II,1,4.
7. See Prv 8:35 LXX.
8. See 1 S 28:7-19.

2 (29). One Book In Answer To The Letter Of Mani Known as *The Foundation*
(*Contra Epistolam Manichaei Quam Vocant Fundamenti Liber Unus*)[9]

The book in answer to the letter of Mani known as *The Foundation* refutes only its beginnings. But, where it seemed appropriate, annotations were added to other parts of it that undermine the whole [letter] and that would serve as reminders if there were ever time to write against all of it.

This book begins in this way: "The one true omnipotent God."

3 (30). One Book On The Christian Combat
(*De Agone Christiano Liber Unus*)[10]

The book on the Christian combat was composed in simple language for brothers who were not educated in Latin. It contains the rule of faith and precepts for living.

In it I wrote, "Let us not listen to those who deny the future resurrection of the flesh and who cite what the apostle Paul says, *Flesh and blood shall not possess the kingdom of God* (1 Cor 15:50). They do not understand what the Apostle himself says, *This corruptible must put on incorruption, and this mortal must put on immortality* (1 Cor 15:53), for, when this has happened, it will no longer be flesh and blood but a heavenly body."[11] This must not be taken to mean that the substance of the flesh will not exist, but by the term *flesh and blood* the Apostle must be understood to have indicated the corruption of flesh and blood, which will certainly not exist in that kingdom, where the flesh will be incorruptible. It can also be understood differently, however, so that we take the Apostle as having referred to the works of flesh and blood as *flesh and blood* and as having said that those who

---

9. Written in 396 or 397.
10. Written between 396 and 397.
11. 32,34.

are constant in their love for such things will not possess the kingdom of God.

This book begins in this way: "The crown of victory."

4 (31). FOUR BOOKS ON TEACHING CHRISTIANITY
(De Doctrina Christiana Libri Quattuor)[12]

1. When I found that the books on teaching Christianity were incomplete, I preferred to complete them rather than to leave them as they were and move on to other things that needed revising. Accordingly, I finished the third [book], which had been written as far as the place where the text from the gospel is cited about the woman who hid yeast in three measures of meal until it was all leavened.[13] I also added a final book, and I finished the work in four books, of which the first three are useful for understanding the scriptures, while the fourth is about how things that we understand should be set forth.

2. In the second book, concerning the author of the book that many call the Wisdom of Solomon, namely, that Jesus Sirach wrote it just as he did Ecclesiasticus,[14] I afterwards learned that this was not as agreed upon as it was said to be by me, and in all probability the book's author is not discoverable.

When I said, "The authority of the Old Testament is confined within these forty-four books,"[15] I referred to the Old Testament according to the Church's customary way of speaking. The Apostle, however, seems to refer only to what was given on Mount Sinai as the Old Testament.[16]

And when I said that Saint Ambrose solved a chronological question by making Plato and Jeremiah contemporaries, my memory failed me.[17] For what the bishop said on this subject

---

12. Begun in 395-396 and completed about 426, when Augustine was in the process of composing the *Revisions*, as is evident from *Revisions* II,4,1.
13. See Lk 13:21. See III,25,35.
14. II,8,13. On Augustine's uncertainty about the Book of Wisdom see also *Revisions* II,20.
15. II,8,13.
16. See Gal 4:24.
17. II,28,43.

can be read in the book of his that he wrote, *The Sacraments, or Philosophy.*[18]

This work begins in this way: "There are certain precepts."

5 (32). Two Books Against The Party Of Donatus
(Contra Partem Donati Libri Duo)[19]

There are two books of mine entitled *Against the Party of Donatus*. In the first of them I said that I did not favor the use of violent force, through the action of any secular authority, in bringing schismatics into communion. To be sure, I did not favor it at the time because I did not yet have any experience either of how much evil they would dare to carry out when their wickedness went unpunished or of how much attentive discipline could profit those who needed to be changed for the better.

This work begins in this way: "Because the Donatists...us."

6 (33). Thirteen Books Of Confessions
(Confessionum Libri Tredecim)[20]

1. The thirteen books of my confessions praise the just and good God for both the bad and the good that I did, and they draw a person's mind and emotions towards him. As for myself, that is how they affected me when they were being written, and that is how they affect me when they are being read. What others may think about them is up to them, but I know that they have pleased and do please many of the brothers a great deal. The first to the tenth [books] were written about me and the three others about the holy scriptures, from what is written, *In*

---

18. This work is mentioned and briefly quoted in the *Answer to Julian* II,5,14-6,15.7,20, where it is given the title *The Sacrament of Regeneration, or Philosophy*. It has not survived in its entirety. Whatever he may or may not have said in *The Sacraments, or Philosophy* about Plato and Jeremiah, Ambrose did occasionally say, however, that Plato was exposed to Old Testament teachings. See *Abraham* II, 7,37; *Noah and the Ark* 8,24; *Flight from the World* 8,51; *Exposition of Psalm 118* [119], sermon 18,4.
19. This work, which no longer exists, must have been written about 396.
20. Written between 397 and 401.

the beginning God made heaven and earth (Gn 1:1), up to *the repose of the sabbath* (Gn 2:2).

2. In the fourth book I acknowledged the wretchedness of my soul at the death of a friend and said that our soul had somehow become one out of two. "And therefore," I said, "I perhaps feared dying, lest he die utterly whom I had so greatly loved."[21] This seems to me to be a frivolous rather than a serious assertion, although its foolishness is somewhat tempered by the "perhaps" that was included.

And in the thirteenth book what I said, "The firmament was created between the spiritual waters above and the bodily ones below,"[22] was not said with sufficient reflection; the issue is in any event very obscure.

This work begins in this way: "You are great, Lord."

7 (34). THIRTY-THREE BOOKS
IN ANSWER TO FAUSTUS, A MANICHEAN
(Contra Faustum Manichaeum Libri Triginta Tres)[23]

1. I wrote a vast work against Faustus, a Manichean, who blasphemed against the law and the prophets and their God and the incarnation of Christ, and said that the writings of the New Testament, by which he stands convicted, were falsified. I set out his own words and gave my answers in return. There are thirty-three discussions. Why should I not just as well call them books? For, even if some of them are very short, still they are books. One of them, on the other hand, in which we defend the life of the patriarchs against his calumnies, is longer than almost any of my books.[24]

2. In the third book, then, as I was addressing the question as to how Joseph could have had two fathers,[25] I actually said that

21. IV,6,11.
22. XIII,32,47.
23. Written between 398 and 400. Faustus was a Manichean bishop; he and Augustine's encounter with him during his Manichean phase are described in *Confessions* V,3,3.6,10-7,13.
24. XXII.
25. See Mt 1:16; Lk 3:23. This issue is also brought up in *Revisions* II,12; 16; 55,3.

he was born of the one and adopted by the other. I should also have mentioned the kind of adoption, however, since it sounds as though the other father adopted him while he was alive. But the law also allowed for the adoption of sons on behalf of the dead, when it ordered that a brother should take his dead brother's wife, if he had no sons, and raise up descendents for his deceased brother from her.[26] That is a much simpler explanation of the two fathers of a single person. These were two brothers with a single mother in whose case it happened that the one—that is, Jacob, by whom Matthew narrates that Joseph was begotten—took the wife of the other, who was dead and who was called Heli. He begot him for his own brother, born of the same mother, whose son Luke says was Joseph, although it was not really a case of having been begotten but rather of having been adopted. This is to be found in a letter of those who wrote about this matter after the Lord's ascension, when it was still fresh in their memory. Africanus even mentioned the name of the woman who begot Jacob, the father of Joseph, from her previous husband, Matthan, who (according to Matthew) was the father of Jacob and the grandfather of Joseph, and who from her next husband, Melchi, begot Heli, by whom Joseph was adopted.[27] I had not yet read this, in fact, when I was responding to Faustus, but nonetheless I could not doubt that it could have been the case that, by way of adoption, one person had two fathers.

   3. In the twelfth and thirteenth [books][28] there was a discussion about Noah's second son, who was called Ham, which suggested that he was cursed by his father not in his son Canaan, as scripture shows,[29] but in himself.

---

26. See Dt 25:5-6; Mt 22:24 par.
27. See Julius Africanus, *Letter to Aristides* 3.9-15. In this letter Africanus (died after 240) tries to reconcile the genealogies of Matthew and Luke. He is apparently one of several "who wrote about this matter," although he did not do so soon after the Lord's ascension.
28. XII,23; XIII,10.
29. See Gn 9:25.

In the fourteenth [book][30] the sun and the moon were spoken of as though they had intelligence and therefore tolerated their foolish worshipers, although the words there could be taken as having been transferred from what does have a soul to what does not have a soul, in the manner of speaking that is called metaphor in Greek. That is how the sea is written about, *which roars in its mother's womb while wanting to break forth* (Jb 38:8), even though of course it does not have a will.

In the twenty-ninth [book] I said, "Perish the thought that there should be in the members of the saints, even in their genitals, anything wicked. They are said to be dishonorable, to be sure, because they do not have the kind of beauty that those members have which are located in full view."[31] But the reason that was given in other later writings of ours[32] is more likely—that the Apostle also called them dishonorable on account of the law in our members that fights against the law of our mind,[33] which is the result of sin and not the way our nature was first made.

This work begins in this way: "There was a certain Faustus."

8 (35). Two Books In Answer To Felix, A Manichean (*Contra Felicem Manichaeum Libri Duo*)[34]

I debated on two days in church, in the presence of the people, against a certain Manichean by the name of Felix. He had come to Hippo in order to disseminate that same error, for he was one of their teachers; although unschooled in the liberal arts, he was nonetheless craftier than Fortunatus.[35] The two books are official ecclesiastical records but are counted among my books, and in the second of them there is a discussion about the free

---

30. XIV,12.
31. XXIX,4.
32. See *The City of God* XXII,19.
33. See Rom 7:23; 1 Cor 12:23.
34. This debate was held on December 7, 404, as indicated at the beginning of the work. Apart from what we learn here, the identity of Felix is uncertain.
35. See *Revisions* I,16.

choice of the will for the accomplishing of either bad or good. But, because such was the man with whom we were dealing, we were not constrained by any necessity to discuss grace more extensively, by which we truly become the free persons of whom it is written, *If the Son has set you free, then you will truly be free* (Jn 8:36).

This work begins in this way: "When Honorius Augustus was consul for the sixth time, on the seventh day before the Ides of December."

9 (36). One Book On The Nature Of The Good
(De Natura Boni Liber Unus)[36]

There is a book on the nature of the good against the Manicheans, where it is shown that God is an immutable nature and the highest good; and that other natures, whether spiritual or bodily, are from him, and that all of them, insofar as they are natures, are good; and where evil is from and what it is; and how many evils the Manicheans assign to the nature of the good and how many good things to the nature of evil—these being the natures that their error has devised.

This book begins in this way: "God is the highest good, than which none is higher."

10 (37). One Book In Answer To Secundinus,
A Manichean
(Contra Secundinum Manichaeum Liber Unus)[37]

A certain Secundinus—not one of those whom the Manicheans call "elect," but one of those whom they call "hearers,"[38] whom I

---

36. Written probably in 404-405.
37. Written probably after 404. Secundinus was a Roman Manichean. His letter to Augustine, which is included with its response, is marked by its courteous tone, as Augustine himself comments.
38. Augustine distinguishes between hearers and elect in *Confessions* V,10,18. The hearers were roughly equivalent to catechumens, while the elect were fully committed

did not actually know by sight—wrote to me as though he were my friend, respectfully reproaching me for opposing that heresy in my writings, and admonishing me not to do so and encouraging me rather to be a follower of it, along with a defense of his faith and a rejection of the Catholic faith. I responded to this. But, because I did not put down at the beginning of the same work who wrote it or to whom it was written, it is not listed among my letters but among my books. His letter was also transcribed there at the beginning. The title of this volume of mine is *An Answer to Secundinus, a Manichean*, which, in my opinion, I greatly prefer to all the others that I was able to write against that plague.

This book begins in this way: "Your good will in my regard, which is obvious from your letter."

11 (38). One Book In Answer To Hilary
(Contra Hilarum Liber Unus)[39]

Meanwhile a certain Hilary, a former tribune and a Catholic layman, was angry (I do not know why) at the ministers of God, as often happens. Declaring that it should not be done, he railed with all the abusiveness that he could muster against the practice (which had started in Carthage at the time) of singing the hymns from the Book of Psalms at the altar either before the offering or when what had been offered was being distributed to the people.[40] I responded to this at the insistence of the brothers, and the book itself is called *An Answer to Hilary.*

This book begins in this way: "Those who say that mentioning the Old Testament."

Manicheans.

39. This work, which no longer exists, must have been written in the early 400s. Hilary (Hilarus or Hilarius) is otherwise unknown.

40. See *Confessions* IX,7,15 on the use of psalmody in the western Church. Here it is said that psalms were sung before the eucharistic prayer or during communion, at the distribution of the consecrated species, *pace* Bardy in BA XII,579, n. 45 ("lorsqu'on distribuait au peuple le pain qui n'avait pas été consacré"), repeated in NBA II,167, n. 29.

12 (39). QUESTIONS ON THE GOSPELS, IN TWO BOOKS
(Quaestiones Evangeliorum, Libri Duo)[41]

These are some explanations of certain passages from the Gospel according to Matthew, and likewise others from that according to Luke; the former were published in one book and the latter in a second. The title of this work is *Questions on the Gospels*. Why these are the only explanations of the aforesaid gospel books that are included among my books, and which ones they are, my prologue is sufficient to indicate; there those same questions are added and numbered in such a way that anyone who pays attention to the numbers will find whatever he wants to read.

In the first book, then, where it says, "The Lord announced his passion to two of his disciples by themselves,"[42] the faultiness of the codex caused us to err, for what is written is not *two* but *twelve*.

In the second book, while seeking to explain how Joseph— whose spouse is called the Virgin Mary—could have two fathers, I said, "What is suggested, that a brother took his dead brother's wife, so that he would raise up descendents for him in keeping with the law,[43] is flawed, because the law ordered that he who would be born was to take the name of the deceased."[44] This is not true, for the law commanded that the name of the deceased, which is spoken of, was to be used so that he would be called his son, not so that he would take his name.

This work begins in this way: "This work was not written in such a way."

---

41. Written about 400.
42. I,27. See Mt 20:17 par.
43. See Dt 25:5-6; Mt 22:24 par.
44. II,5. This issue is also brought up in *Revisions* II,7,2; 16; 55,3.

13 (40). Notes On Job, In One Book
(Annotationes In Iob, Liber Unus)[45]

I can hardly say whether the book entitled *Notes on Job* ought to be considered mine or whether it is the product of those who, to the degree that they were able and wanted to do so, gathered my marginal jottings from a codex into a single collection. They are appealing to the very few who understand. When they do not understand many things, however, they will certainly be annoyed, because the words themselves that are being explained are often not written out in such a way that what is being explained is clear. In addition to that, such obscurity accompanies the brevity of the comments that the reader can scarcely tolerate it, and he has to pass over a large number of things that are unintelligible. Finally, I found the work itself so full of mistakes in our codexes that I was unable to correct it, nor would I wish it to be said that I had published it, except that I know that the brothers possess it, and their zeal could not be denied.

This book begins in this way: "And great were his works upon the earth."

14 (41). One Book
On Instructing Beginners In Faith
(De Catechizandis Rudibus Liber Unus)[46]

There is also a book of ours on instructing beginners in faith which has that very title. In that book I said, "The angel who, along with his other attendant spirits, abandoned God's obedience through pride and became the devil did no harm of any sort to God but to himself, for God knows what to do with the souls that abandon him."[47] It would have been better to say

---

45. Probably written in 399.
46. Written between 399 and 405.
47. 18,30.

"the spirits that abandon him," because it was angels that were at issue.

This book begins in this way: "You asked me, brother Deogratias."

15 (42). FIFTEEN BOOKS ON THE TRINITY
(De Trinitate Libri Quindecim)[48]

1. I wrote fifteen books on the Trinity, which is God, over the course of a number of years. But when I had not yet finished the twelfth of them, and I was holding on to them longer than those who vehemently desired to have them were able to bear, they were taken from me in a less corrected state than they should have been or could have been, when I would have wanted to publish them. I found this out afterwards and, because other copies of them remained in our possession, decided not to publish them myself at the time but to keep them as they were, so that in some other work of mine I could relate what happened to me in their regard. Urged on by the brothers, however, whom I could not resist, I corrected them as much as I thought they should be corrected, and I completed and published them. At the point where they began I added a letter that I wrote to Aurelius, the venerable bishop of the church of Carthage;[49] it serves as a kind of prologue, and in it I explained what happened, and what, in my own thoughts, I had wanted to do, and what I did do out of a compelling love for the brothers.[50]

2. In the eleventh of these books, when a visible body was under discussion, I said, "That is why it is foolish to love it."[51] This was said in reference to that love whereby something is

---

48. Begun around 400 and completed in the early 420s.
49. Letter 174. Aurelius, a long-time friend of Augustine and a person of great importance in the African church, was bishop of Carthage from the early 390s until his death in 430.
50. "Out of a compelling love for the brothers": *fratrum caritate compellente. Fratrum* is translated here as an objective genitive, but it could also be translated as a subjective genitive, in which case it could be rendered "as a result of the brothers' loving urging."
51. XI,5,9.

loved in such a way that the one who loves it thinks that he is happy when he is enjoying it. For it is not foolish for someone to love a bodily form to the praise of the creator, so that he is truly happy because he enjoys the creator himself.[52]

Again, in the same book I said, "I have no memory of a four-footed bird because I have not seen one, but it is very easy to form an image of one by adding two other feet, just like ones that I have seen, to any winged creature such as I have seen."[53] When I said this I could not recall the four-footed flying creatures that the law mentions. Neither, with regard to feet, does this take into consideration the two hind legs with which locusts jump, which it calls clean and therefore distinguishes from the sorts of unclean flying creatures that do not jump with their hind legs—for example, beetles. All flying creatures of this kind are referred to as four-footed in the law. [54]

3. In the twelfth, my explanation of the Apostle's words, when he says, *Every sin whatsoever that a man commits is outside the body* (1 Cor 6:18), does not satisfy me. Nor do I think that the words, *He who commits fornication sins against his own body* (1 Cor 6:18), should be understood as though someone who does something for the sake of acquiring things that are known through the body, so as to locate his own ultimate good in them, does such a thing. For this includes far more sins than that fornication which is perpetrated through unlawful sexual union, which it appears that the Apostle was talking about when he said this.

This work, apart from the letter that was later added to its beginning, starts in this way: "The person who is about to read what we are discussing in regard to the Trinity."

---

52. Augustine presupposes here the knowledge of a distinction of his own making between use and enjoyment, which is elaborated in *Teaching Christianity* I,3,3-40,44: only God may be enjoyed, and all other things are to be used to attain to God.
53. XI,10,17.
54. See Lv 11:20-23.

16 (43). Four Books On The Agreement Among The Evangelists

(De Consensu Evangelistarum Libri Quattuor)[55]

During these same years, when I was dictating the books on the Trinity in piecemeal fashion, I also continually exerted myself in the writing of others, which I interposed at various times. Among them are the four books on the agreement among the evangelists, [written] because of those who misrepresent them as though they were in disagreement. The first of these books was composed in answer to those who give the impression that they greatly honor Christ as a wise man, or pretend to do so, and do not want to put their trust in the gospel because they[56] were not written by him but by his disciples, who they think erroneously ascribed to him a divinity whereby he was believed to be God.

In that book I said, "The people of the Hebrews began from Abraham,"[57] and it is certainly also believable that the Hebrews are thought to have been called something like Abrahews. But they are more correctly understood to have been called something like Heberews after a man named Heber. I have discussed this matter enough in the sixteenth book of *The City of God.*[58]

In the second [book], when I was dealing with the two fathers of Joseph, I said that he was begotten by the one and adopted by the other.[59] But it should have been said that he was adopted in accordance with the law[60] *for* the one who had died, which is more believable, because he who begot him had taken his mother, the wife of his deceased brother.

Again, I said, "But Luke goes back to David himself through Nathan, and it was through that prophet that God forgave his

---

55. Probably written in late 404.
56. Augustine has gone from the singular ("gospel") to the plural ("they").
57. I,14,21.
58. See *The City of God* XVI,3.11.
59. II,3,5. This issue is also raised in *Revisions* II,7,2; 12; 55,3.
60. See Dt 25:5-6.

sin."[61] I ought to have said "through the prophet of this name," lest anyone think that this was the same person when it was someone else, although that was what he too was called .[62]

This work begins in this way: "Among all the divine authorities."

17 (44). THREE BOOKS IN ANSWER TO THE LETTER OF PARMENIAN
(Contra Epistolam Parmeniani Libri Tres)[63]

In three books in answer to a letter of Parmenian, the bishop of the Donatists of Carthage and a successor of Donatus,[64] an important question is addressed and answered concerning the Church that is spread over the whole earth,[65] against which they have created a schism through their false accusations. The discussion has to do with whether bad persons contaminate good ones when they are joined together and communicate in the same sacraments,[66] and with how they do not have a contaminating effect.

In the third of these books there was a discussion as to how the Apostle's words should be taken, *Remove the wicked person from among yourselves* (1 Cor 5:13), and what I said, that everyone should remove the wicked thing from himself,[67] is not how it should be understood. It should be taken to mean, rather, that a wicked person should be removed from among good persons, which is done through ecclesiastical disciplining. This is quite clear in the Greek language, where it is unambiguously written in such a way that a wicked person and not a wicked thing is to

---

61. II,4,12. See Lk 3:31.
62. Augustine expresses the same concern in *Revisions* I,26, question 61.
63. Written about 400.
64. Parmenian was the Donatist bishop of Carthage from 362 until 390 or 391.
65. In comparing Donatism with Catholicism, Augustine often notes that Catholicism is universal, whereas Donatism is confined to North Africa. As though to emphasize the aspect of universality, he sometimes refers to the Catholic Church simply by the Latin word *catholica*—"the universal one." See I,14,6; II,18; 25.
66. The Donatist position was that the Church should not abide the presence of bad persons, who would contaminate the good.
67. III,1,2.

be understood, although I also responded to Parmenian with that understanding in mind.[68]

This work begins in this way: "Many things indeed, at other times, against the Donatists."

18 (45). SEVEN BOOKS ON BAPTISM
(De Baptismo Libri Septem)[69]

I wrote seven books on baptism in answer to the Donatists, who were endeavoring to defend themselves by the authority of the most blessed bishop and martyr Cyprian.[70] In them I taught that there is nothing as powerful for refuting the Donatists and for closing their mouths completely, so that they may not defend their schism against the Catholic Church,[71] as the letters and the life of Cyprian.

Wherever in these books, however, I mentioned *the Church that has no spot or wrinkle* (Eph 5:27),[72] it must not be understood as though that is already the case, but it is being readied to be so, when it will also appear glorious. For now, because of a certain ignorance and weakness on the part of its members, the whole [Church] has cause to pray every day, *Forgive us our debts* (Mt 6:12).[73]

In the fourth book, when I said that suffering could take the place of baptism,[74] the example of the thief[75] that I offered was not quite apropos, because it is uncertain that he was not baptized.[76]

---

68. Augustine's problem here is based on the Latin translation of the biblical Greek. The Latin *auferte malum* can mean either "remove the wicked thing" or "remove the wicked person." The original Greek, however, which Augustine had not consulted (and which perhaps he would not have understood), makes it clear that a person and not a thing is being referred to.
69. Written about 400.
70. On Cyprian see p. 28, n. 18.
71. Augustine simply uses the term *catholica*, as he often does, for the Church. See also *Revisions* I,14,6; II,25; and p. 126, n. 65.
72. I,17,26; III,18,23; IV,3,5; VII,10,19.
73. See p. 41, n. 92.
74. IV,22,29.
75. See Lk 23:40-43.
76. See *Revisions* I,26, question 62; II,55,3.

In the seventh book I followed Cyprian's understanding of the gold and silver vessels that are found in a great house. These he understood as good, whereas the wooden and clay ones were bad; to the former he referred these words, *Some indeed unto honor*, while to the latter he referred these words, *But others unto shamefulness* (2 Tm 2:20).[77] But I am more favorable to what I discovered and saw afterwards in Tyconius, which is that it should be understood that some of each are *unto honor*, not only the gold and silver [vessels], and, again, that some of each are *unto shamefulness*, not only, to be sure, the wooden and clay ones.[78]

This work begins in this way: "In the books answering the letter of Parmenian."

19 (46). ONE BOOK IN ANSWER TO WHAT CENTURIUS, ONE OF THE DONATISTS, PRESENTED (*Contra Quod Attulit Centurius A Donatistis Liber Unus)*[79]

While we were involved in numerous debates with the party of Donatus, a certain layman, who at the time was one of them, presented against us in church several (albeit few) items in spoken and written form as proof-texts that they think are favorable to their cause. I responded to them very briefly. The title of this pamphlet is *An Answer to What Centurius, One of the Donatists, Presented*, and it begins in this way: "You say that by what was written by Solomon, *Keep away from alien water"* (Prv 9:18 LXX).[80]

---

77. See Cyprian, Letter 54,3.
78. See Tyconius, *The Seven Rules* 7 (PL XVIII,63). Tyconius was a Donatist scriptural exegete whose scholarship Augustine esteemed.
79. This text, composed in 400 or 401, no longer exists.
80. This would have been one of the proof texts offered by Centurius. *Baptism* VI,12,18 notes that Prv 9:18 LXX was cited by a Donatist bishop on behalf of the Donatist view of the invalidity of heretical baptism.

20 (47). Two Books In Response To The Questions Of Januarius
(Ad Inquisitiones Ianuarii Libri Duo)[81]

The two books whose title is *Responses to the Questions of Januarius* contain many discussions on the sacraments that the Church practices, whether universally or locally—that is, not uniformly in every place. They could not cover everything, but they are a sufficient response to what was asked. Of these books the first is a letter; at its beginning it states who is writing to whom. But this work is numbered among my books because the next [book], which does not have our names, is much longer, and many more things are treated in it.

In the first [book], then, it did not occur to me that what I said about the manna—that it tasted in each person's mouth as he himself wished it to[82]—could not be demonstrated by any text apart from the Book of Wisdom,[83] which the Jews do not accept as having canonical authorship.[84] Yet that is what it was able to be for those who believed, not for those who murmured against God and who would never have desired other food[85] if the manna had had the taste that they wanted.[86]

This work begins in this way: "In answer to what you asked me."

21 (48). One Book On The Work Of Monks
(De Opere Monachorum Liber Unus)[87]

There was a problem that compelled me to write a book on the work of monks—namely, that when there began to be monas-

---

81. These two books, written about 400, appear in the collection of Augustine's letters as Letters 54 and 55. Januarius was a Catholic layman who had written at least two letters, now lost, to Augustine.
82. Letter 54,3,4.
83. See Wis 16:21.
84. On Augustine's uncertainty about the Book of Wisdom see also *Revisions* II,4,2.
85. See Nm 11:4-6.
86. Inasmuch as the Book of Wisdom is a somewhat questionable source on the subject of the taste of the manna, Augustine justifies his position by common sense or logic.
87. Written around 400.

teries in Carthage, some [monks] were supporting themselves by their own hands in obedience to the Apostle,[88] while others wanted to live off the gifts of the devout. These latter, who engaged in no work whereby they would have, or supply themselves with, the things that they needed, thought and boasted that they were instead fulfilling the gospel precept in which the Lord says, *Consider the birds of the air and the lilies of the field* (Mt 6:26.28). As a result of this, tumultuous disagreements started up even among laypersons with a lowlier vocation who were nevertheless fervent in their zeal, and the Church was agitated by the whole affair, with some people taking one position and others another. Moreover, some of those who said that they were not supposed to work had long hair, which served to add to the dissension, in proportion to the zeal of the parties, between those on one side who condemned this and those on the other who excused it.[89] On this account the venerable old man Aurelius, the bishop of the church of that city,[90] commanded me to write something on the subject, and I did.

This book begins in this way: "At your command, holy brother Aurelius."

22 (49). ONE BOOK ON THE EXCELLENCE OF MARRIAGE
(De Bono Coniugali Liber Unus)[91]

1. Jovinian's heresy enjoyed such prestige in the city of Rome, because it equated the merit of consecrated virgins with married purity, that he was even said to have dragged down into matrimony several nuns about whose purity no suspicion had preceded. He would urge them on especially with this argument, saying, "Are

88. See 1 Thes 4:11.
89. Long hair on men is deplored in 1 Cor 11:14. Thus those who neither worked nor wore their hair short were disregarding the apostle Paul on two counts.
90. On Aurelius see note p. 122, n. 49.
91. Written about 401. Jovinian (died before 406), whose "heresy" occasioned this book, promoted the notion that there was no spiritual inequality between married persons and consecrated virgins, whether men or women, and stressed the overriding importance of baptism, shared by both ascetics and non-ascetics. He also questioned the perpetual virginity of Mary. Jerome's most blustering polemic, *Against Jovinian*, was written to counter his positions.

you better than Sarah, then, or better than Susanna or Anne?"[92]
And when he cited other texts that referred to the most distinguished women of holy scripture, they were unable to think that
they themselves were better than they, nor even their equal. In this
way he also broke down the holy celibacy of holy men by mentioning and making comparisons with the patriarchs, who were married.[93] The holy church that is there resisted this monster with the
greatest faith and firmness, but those arguments of his had survived
in the gossip and whisperings of certain persons, and no one dared
to address them openly. But this concealed and unexpected poison
had to be confronted with the means that the Lord provided, especially since it was being bruited about that no response could be
made to Jovinian that would praise rather than demean marriage.
For that reason I published this book, entitled *The Excellence of
Marriage*. In it an important question was deferred until later concerning the propagation of children before human beings merited
death by sinning, because sexual union seems to be a matter for
bodies subject to death. But this is explained later, and I think as
much as necessary, in other writings of ours.[94]

2. In a certain passage I said, "What food is to the health of
man, sexual union is to the health of the race, and both are not
without fleshly enjoyment; when, however, thanks to the brake of
temperance, they have been regulated and brought back to their
natural use, there can be no wanton excess."[95] This was said because there is no good wanton excess and no right use of wanton
excess. For just as it is bad to use good things badly, so it is good
to use bad things well. I discussed this matter in greater detail on
other occasions, especially against the recent Pelagian heretics.[96]

---

92. For Sarah, the wife of Abraham, see Gn 12:1-23:2. For Susanna see Dn 13. According to
    a tradition dating to the second century, Anne was the name of the mother of Mary, but
    Jovinian could also be referring to Hannah, the mother of Samuel (see 1 S 1:1-2:10).
93. E.g., Abraham, Isaac, Jacob.
94. See *The City of God* XIV,21-22.
95. 16,18. "Wanton excess": *libido*.
96. See *Marriage and Desire* II,21,36; *Answer to Julian* III,7,16; V,16,60. "The recent
    Pelagian heretics": see p. 45, n. 104.

I do not entirely approve of what I said about Abraham: "Out of obedience Father Abraham, who was not without a wife, was ready to be without his only son, who would have been slain by him."[97] For, if he had been slain, it must be believed instead that he believed that his son would soon be returned to him by being raised up, as can be read in the Epistle to the Hebrews.[98]

This book begins in this way: "Since each person is a part of the human race."

23 (50). ONE BOOK ON HOLY VIRGINITY
(De Sancta Virginitate Liber Unus)[99]

After I wrote about the excellence of marriage, it was expected that I would write about holy virginity. I did not delay, and in one volume I showed as well as I could how great a gift of God it was and with what humility it needed to be maintained.

This book begins in this way: "I recently published a book about the excellence of marriage."

24 (51). TWELVE BOOKS
ON THE LITERAL MEANING OF GENESIS
(De Genesi Ad Litteram Libri Duodecim)[100]

1. During the same period I wrote twelve books on Genesis, from its beginning until Adam was expelled from paradise and *a flaming sword was placed to guard the way to the tree of life* (Gn 3:24). But when eleven books had been completed up to that point, I added a twelfth, in which there was a more detailed discussion of paradise. The title of those books is *The Literal Meaning of Genesis*, and hence it is not concerned with allegorical meanings but with the proper significance of actual facts. In this work there are more questions than answers, and of those answers relatively few

97. 23,31.
98. See Heb 11:19.
99. Written about 401.
100. Begun between 399 and 404 and published in 416.

are settled, while the rest have been proposed in such a way that they still need to be examined. I began these books in fact after *The Trinity* but finished them before [I finished it]. Consequently I have reviewed them now in the order in which I began them.

2. In the fifth book and elsewhere in those books I said, "Of the seed to whom it was promised that it would be *ordained by angels in the hand of the mediator*" (Gal 3:19).[101] This is not what the Apostle says, in keeping with the more reliable codexes that I looked at afterwards, especially the Greek ones, since through a mistranslation many Latin codexes use the word "seed." For it is the law that is being spoken of.

What I said in the sixth book, "Because of his sin Adam destroyed the image of God, according to which he had been made,"[102] must not be understood as though none of it remained in him, but that it was so deformed that it needed to be refashioned.

In the twelfth [book], regarding the nether regions, it seems to me that I ought to have taught that they are beneath the earth rather than to have explained why they are believed to be or said to be beneath the earth, as though that were not the case.[103]

This work begins in this way: "All of divine scripture is divided into two parts."

25 (52). THREE BOOKS IN ANSWER TO THE WRITINGS OF PETILIAN
(Contra Litteras Petiliani Libri Tres)[104]

Before I finished the books on the Trinity and the books on the literal meaning of Genesis there was an urgent need, which I

---

101. V,19,38; IX,16,30.
102. VI,27,28.
103. XII,33,62; 34,66. See also *Revisions* I,5,3 and p. 36, n. 69. Augustine was apparently so certain about the nether regions' location beneath the surface of the earth that he thought that his explanation might have suggested that he was doubtful about the matter or that this was not a settled teaching of the Church.
104. Probably begun around 400 and completed around 403. Petilian was the Donatist bishop of Constantina, or Cirta, in Numidia. This is the first of two works intended to respond to him. See also *Revisions* II,34.

could not defer, to respond to the writings of Petilian, a Donatist, that he wrote against the Catholic Church.[105] And in answer to this matter I wrote three volumes. In the first of them I responded as rapidly and as truthfully as I could to the first section of a letter of his that he wrote to his own people, because not all of it had come into our hands but only the first section of it, which is brief. It is also a letter addressed to our people, but it is listed among my books because the other two that are involved in the same matter are books. Afterwards, in fact, we found the whole [letter of Petilian], and I responded to it as carefully as I had to the Manichean Faustus by placing what he wrote first, in segments, under his name and giving my response to each segment under mine. But what I had written first reached Petilian, before we found the whole [letter], and in his anger he attempted to respond, saying whatever he pleased against me; as far as the issue itself was concerned, however, he was utterly deficient. While this could be very easily observed when the writings of each of us were compared, nonetheless, on account of those who were slower, I took care to demonstrate it by responding, and that is how a third book was added to this same work of ours.

This work begins in the first book in this way: "You know that we have often wanted."

In the second in this way: "In the first sections of Petilian's letter."

And in the third in this way: "I have read your letter, Petilian."

26 (53). FOUR BOOKS IN ANSWER TO CRESCONIUS,
A GRAMMARIAN OF THE DONATIST PARTY
*(Ad Cresconium Grammaticum Partis Donati
Libri Quattuor)*[106]

When Cresconius, a certain Donatist grammarian, saw the letter of mine in which I refuted the first sections of the letter

105. "Catholic Church": *catholica*. See also *Revisions* II,18 and p. 125, n. 65.
106. Written in 405 or 406. Cresconius was a friend of Petilian and a native of Proconsular Africa.

of Petilian that had come into my hands at the time, he thought that he ought to respond to me, and he wrote to me. I responded to his work in four books in such a way that in fact I completed in three everything that the response required. When, however, given the situation of the Maximianists,[107] whom they [i.e., the Donatists] condemned as schismatics, and the fact that they took some of them back in their ecclesiastical positions and did not repeat the baptism that was performed by them outside their own communion, I saw that a response could be made to everything that he wrote, and I also added a fourth book in which I exposed this very matter as well as I could, carefully and with evidence.[108] But when I wrote these four books, the emperor Honorius had already laid down laws against the Donatists.[109]

This work begins in this way: "When, unbeknownst to me, my writings were able to make their way to you, Cresconius."

27 (54). One Book Of Proofs And Testimonies In Answer To The Donatists
(Probationum Et Testimoniorum Contra Donatistas Liber Unus)[110]

After [I had written] these things, I saw to it that the necessary documentation against their error and on behalf of Catholic truth, whether ecclesiastical or from civil proceedings or from the canonical scriptures, was brought to the attention of the Donatists. And first I promised them that they themselves might request to see these things, depending on their availability. When they came

---

107. The Maximianists, so called after a Donatist bishop, broke away from the main body of the Donatists in the 390s; some were still active into the early 400s. Our information about them comes mainly from the *Answer to Cresconius* III-IV; *Exposition of Psalm* 36, sermon 2,19-23.
108. The usual practice of the Donatists when receiving converts into their church was to rebaptize those who had been baptized by non-Donatists and, if they held an ecclesiastical rank, to discount it. Augustine notes this discrepancy on their part in the case of the Maximianists.
109. These laws are mentioned in III,43,47 and were promulgated in 405.
110. This work, which must have been written about 406, has not survived.

into the hands of a few of them, there was somebody or other who wrote against them anonymously, claiming to be a Donatist, just as though that was what he was called. In response to him I wrote another book.[111] But the documentation that I had promised I appended to the same book in which I had promised it; I wished to put both things together, and I published it in such a way that it would be exposed to view and read for the first time on the walls of the basilica that belonged to the Donatists.[112] Its title is *Proofs and Testimonies in Answer to the Donatists.*

In this book we did not put the vindication of Felix of Apthungi, who ordained Caecilian, in the sequence that was later made clear to us, after we had carefully noted the consuls; instead of his having been vindicated after Caecilian, it happened before.[113]

Also, when I recalled the testimony of the apostle Jude, where he says, *These are persons who cut themselves off; they are animal, not possessing the spirit* (Jude 19), I added what the apostle Paul says, *The animal man does not grasp the things that are of the Spirit of God* (1 Cor 2:14). The former, whom schism completely cuts off from the Church, must not be equated with the latter. The same apostle Paul in fact says that the latter are babies in Christ, whom he feeds with milk because they are as yet unable to take solid food.[114] The former, however, must be considered not as babies but as dead and lost, so that, if one of them were to be corrected and joined to the Church, it could rightly be said of him,

---

111. See *Revisions* II,28.
112. I.e., the Donatist church in Hippo.
113. Felix was one of three bishops who ordained Caecilian bishop of Carthage in 311, following the death of his predecessor, Mensurius. Because of Caecilian's unpopularity his ordination was disputed, and about 312 a rival bishop, Maiorinus, was ordained as well. Felix, meanwhile, was accused of having surrendered the scriptures to the Roman authorities during the Great Persecution in 304 which, in the eyes of some, meant that he had apostatized and could not validly ordain Caecilian. The rift between the two parties, that of Caecilian and that of Maiorinus, gave rise to the Donatist schism, Maiorinus being on what would later be known as the Donatist side. In 313 and 314 several Catholic church councils decided in favor of both Caecilian and Felix, and in 316 Caecilian was vindicated by the Emperor Constantine himself. The mention of the consuls refers to the years when the events occurred, since any given year was named after the two consuls in office for that year. See also *Revisions* II,34.
114. See 1 Cor 3:1-2.

He was dead and has come to life; he was lost and has been found (Lk 15:32).

This book begins in this way: "You who fear to be in accord with the Catholic Church."

28 (55). ONE BOOK IN ANSWER TO A CERTAIN DONATIST
(Contra Nescio Quem Donatistam Liber Unus)[115]

The other book that I mentioned above[116] I wanted to be entitled *An Answer to a Certain Donatist*.

Here the chronology of the vindication of the ordainer of Caecilian is likewise incorrect.[117]

Also, what I said, "To the multitude of weeds,[118] by which all heresies are understood," does not have a conjunction where one is needed, for what should have been said was "by which all heresies are *also* understood" or "by which all heresies are understood *as well*." But, as it stands, it sounds as though there are weeds only outside the Church and not also in the Church, although it is itself the kingdom of Christ, from which the angels will gather all causes of offense at its harvest time.[119] Hence the martyr Cyprian also said, "Even if there are seen to be weeds in the Church, still our faith and our charity must not be adversely affected with the result that, because we see that there are weeds in the Church, we ourselves leave the Church."[120] This is the understanding that we too have defended on other occasions,[121] especially in a conference directed against the Donatists, who were present.[122]

This book begins in this way: "We promised that the necessary proofs would be collected in a kind of summary."

---

115. This book, which has been lost, must have been written about 406.
116. See *Revisions* II,27.
117. See *Revisions* II,27 and p. 135, n. 113.
118. See Mt 13:36.
119. See Mt 13:41.
120. Cyprian, Letter 54,3.
121. See *Answer to Cresconius* III,31,35; IV,56,67; *Answer to Gaudentius* II,3,3; *To the Donatists after the Conference* VI,9,20.28.
122. This was very likely the famous Conference of Carthage, held in 411. See p. 145, n. 153.

29 (56). A Notice To The Donatists About The Maximianists, In One Book
(Admonitio Donatistarum De Maximianistis, Liber Unus)[123]

When I saw that, because it was hard for them to read, many people were prevented from learning that the party of the Donatus had no claim whatsoever on reason or truth, I composed a very brief pamphlet. In it I thought that they should be advised only about the Maximianists, and because of the ease of copying it, it would come into the hands of more people, and because of its brevity it would be easier to remember. I gave it the title of *A Notice to the Donatists about the Maximianists.*

This book begins in this way: "Whoever of you are disturbed by the calumnies and accusations of men."

30 (57). One Book On Demonic Divination
(De Divinatione Daemonum Liber Unus)[124]

During the same period, as the result of a certain discussion, I found myself obliged to write a book on demonic divination, which is what its title is.

In a certain passage in it I said, "Demons occasionally learn the dispositions of human beings with the greatest ease, not only when they have been expressed in speech but also when they have been conceived in thought, when certain signals from the soul are expressed in the body."[125] Here I spoke of something very obscure in bolder terms than I should have. For it has been ascertained, thanks to various experiences, that such things come to the notice of the demons. But whether certain signals, obvious to them but hidden from us, emanate from the bodies of persons while they

---

123. This book, which has been lost, was probably written around 406. On the Maximianists see *Revisions* II,26 and p. 134, nn. 107 and 108.
124. Written about 407. As the work's opening line indicates, the discussion that originated the book took place one day during an Easter Octave .
125. 5,9.

are thinking, or whether they know such things by reason of some other spiritual power, can be discovered by human beings either with the greatest difficulty or not at all.

This book begins in this way: "On a certain day, during the holy days of the octave."

31 (58). Six Questions Explained
In Answer To The Pagans

*(Quaestiones Expositae Contra Paganos
Numero Sex)*[126]

Meanwhile six questions were sent to me from Carthage, which were asked by a certain friend whom I wanted to become a Christian and which were to be resolved with a view to the pagans, especially inasmuch as he said that some of them had been proposed by the philosopher Porphyry. I do not think, however, that this was the famous Porphyry the Sicilian, whose reputation is widespread.[127] I assembled the discussions of these questions in a single book, which is not lengthy and whose title is *Six Questions Explained in Answer to the Pagans.*

The first of them is on the resurrection.

The second is on the time of the Christian religion.

The third is on the difference among sacrifices.

The fourth is on what is written: *In the measure that you have measured out it will be measured back to you* (Mt 7:2).

The fifth is on the Son of God according to Solomon.

The sixth is on the prophet Jonah.

In the second of these [discussions] I said, "The salvation of this religion, which alone is true, and by which true salvation is truthfully promised, has never been lacking to anyone who was worthy, and whoever has lacked it was unworthy."[128] I did not say

---

126. Written between 406 and 411. This is listed in Augustine's correspondence as Letter 102, addressed to the priest Deogratias, who had passed on to Augustine questions that had been asked of him by a pagan friend.
127. On the famous Porphyry see p. 34, n. 57.
128. Letter 102,2,15.

this as though someone would be worthy based on his own merits, but in the sense that the Apostle says, *Not because of works but because of the one calling, it was said that the older would serve the younger* (Rom 9:12-13). He declares that this call pertains to God's purpose. Hence he says, *Not according to our works but according to his purpose and grace* (2 Tm 1:9). And hence he says again, *We know that all things work together for the good of those who love God, those who have been called according to his purpose* (Rom 8:28). He says of this call, *That he may make you worthy of his holy call* (2 Thes 1:11).

This book, after the letter that was added later at its beginning,[129] begins in this way: "There are some who are disturbed and ask."

32 (59). A COMMENTARY ON THE EPISTLE OF JAMES TO THE TWELVE TRIBES
(Expositio Epistolae Iacobi Ad Duodecim Tribus)[130]

Among my works I found a commentary on the Epistle of James. While I was engaged in my revisions, I noticed that this was actually the notes for certain passages of it that I had commented on and that were collected into a book, thanks to the diligence of the brothers, who did not want them to remain in the margins of a codex. They are somewhat useful apart from the fact that, when we dictated these things, we did not have a careful translation from the Greek of the epistle that we were reading.

This book begins in this way: *Greetings to the twelve tribes that are in the dispersion* (Jas 1:1).

---

129. Letter 102,1.
130. This lost work was probably written or collated sometime after the previous one. The twelve tribes that appear in the title refer to the twelve tribes of the dispersion that are mentioned in Jas 1:1, which is quoted at the beginning of the work.

33 (60). THREE BOOKS FOR MARCELLINUS ON THE PUNISHMENT AND REMISSION OF SINS AND THE BAPTISM OF INFANTS

(De Peccatorum Meritis Et Remissione Et De Baptismo Parvulorum Ad Marcellinum Libri Tres)[131]

The necessity also arose of having to write in answer to the recent Pelagian heresy,[132] to which I had first responded, when there was a need to do so, not in books but in sermons and conferences,[133] just as any one of our people could have done or should have done. And so, when some questions of theirs had been sent to me from Carthage, which I answered by writing back, I at first wrote three books entitled *The Punishment and Remission of Sins*. In them there is a very lengthy discussion on the baptism of infants because of original sin and on the grace of God whereby we are justified (that is, rendered just), although there is no one in this life who so observes the commandments of justice that, because of his sins, he does not need to say in prayer, *Forgive us our debts* (Mt 6:12).[134] Those who are opposed to all of these things founded a new heresy. In these books, though, I thought that their names should still be passed over in silence, in the hope that in that way they could more easily be corrected. On the other hand, in the third book—which is a letter but which is listed as a book on account of the two with which I thought it should be joined—I mentioned the name of Pelagius himself with a certain amount of praise, because his life was being extolled by many people, and I refuted those things of his

---

131. Written between late 411 and early 412, this is the first of Augustine's numerous anti-Pelagian writings. Marcellinus was a high Roman official, a devout Christian and a close friend of Augustine, who dedicated both this work and *The Spirit and the Letter* to him and also wrote *The City of God* at his suggestion. He presided at the Conference of Carthage in 411 (see p. 145, n. 153) but was executed in 413 for supposedly having taken part in a revolt in Africa.
132. "The recent Pelagian heresy" and also, a few lines later, "a new heresy": see p. 45, n. 104.
133. See Sermons 26-27; 131; 153; 155-156; 158; 165; 169; 174; 176; 181.
134. See *The Punishment and Remission of Sins* II,14,21; 21,25; III,13,23.

that he put in his writings that were not in his own person but that others said and he explained; even so, the heretic defended them afterwards with the most persistent animosity. On account of such assertions, Caelestius, his disciple, had already merited excommunication in Carthage at an episcopal tribunal, at which I was not present.[135]

In the second book I said in a certain passage, "This will be granted to certain persons at the end—that, thanks to a sudden change, they will not sense death."[136] I shall return to this passage for a more careful investigation of the matter. For either they will not die or, by passing from this life into death and from death into eternal life by the most rapid change, as though *in the twinkling of an eye* (1 Cor 15:52), they will not sense death.

This work begins in this way: "Although we are surrounded by great and raging concerns."

34 (61). One Book For Constantine On The One Baptism In Answer To Petilian
(De Unico Baptismo Contra Petilianum Ad Constantinum Liber Unus)[137]

At the same time a certain friend of mine received a book on the one baptism from some Donatist presbyter or other, who indicated that Petilian, a bishop of theirs at Constantine, wrote it. He brought it to me and urgently requested that I respond to it, and that is how it happened. I wanted the book of mine in which I responded to have the same title, which is *The One Baptism.*

---

135. Caelestius, one of two or three people in the Pelagian movement who were as significant as Pelagius himself in defining its theology, was condemned at the Conference of Carthage that was held in 411. Like Pelagius, he was probably of British origin.
136. II,31,50.
137. Written between late 410 and early 411. On Petilian see p. 132, n. 104. The Constantine for whom the book was written is unknown. Since Petilian was bishop of Constantine in North Africa, the title of the book is sometimes taken to read *One Book on the One Baptism in Answer to Petilian of Constantine*, but this seems an unlikely rendering.

In that book I said, "The Emperor Constantine did not deny the Donatists who were accusing Felix of Apthungi, the ordainer of Caecilian, an opportunity to make their accusation, although he had had experience of their calumnies in the trumped-up charges against Caecilian."[138] When I reflected later on the chronology, it was discovered to be different. For the previously-named emperor had Felix's case heard by the proconsul, at which point he was vindicated; and afterwards, when Caecilian had been heard along with his accusers, he himself found him innocent, and it was then that he had experience of their calumnies in their accusations against him. This chronology, established through the consuls, served all the more powerfully to refute the calumnies of the Donatists in that matter and overthrew them completely, which we have shown elsewhere.[139]

This book begins in this way: "Responding to those who have different opinions."

35 (62). ONE BOOK ON THE MAXIMIANISTS IN ANSWER TO THE DONATISTS
(De Maximianistis Contra Donatistis Liber Unus)[140]

Among other things I also wrote a book—not very brief, as before, but lengthy and far more detailed—in answer to the Donatists. In it one may see how the case of the Maximianists of itself completely overthrows that wicked and haughty error of theirs [i.e., of the Donatists] that is opposed to the Catholic Church, because the schism arose out of Donatus's very own party.

This book begins in this way: "We have already said many things, we have already written many things."

---

138. 16,28.
139. See also *Revisions* II,27 and p. 135, n. 113.
140. This work, now lost, was written about 412. On the Maximianists see p. 134, nn. 107 and 108.

36 (63). ONE BOOK FOR HONORATUS
ON THE GRACE OF THE NEW TESTAMENT
(De Gratia Testamenti Novi Ad Honoratum Liber Unus)[141]

At that very time, when we were fiercely struggling against the Donatists and had already begun to struggle against the Pelagians, a certain friend sent me five questions from Carthage and asked that I answer them in writing for him. They are:

"What did those words of the Lord mean, *My God, my God, why have you forsaken me*" (Ps 22:1; Mt 27:46)?

And: "What did the Apostle mean when he said, *So that, rooted and grounded in charity, you may be able to understand, with all the holy ones, what is the breadth and length and the height and depth*" (Eph 3:17-18)?

And: "Who are the five foolish virgins and the five wise ones?"[142]

And: "What is the outer darkness?"[143]

And: "How is this to be understood: *The Word was made flesh*" (Jn 1:14)?

Seeing, however, that the aforesaid recent heresy[144] was inimical to the grace of God, I myself posed a sixth question on the grace of the New Testament. In discussing it (while interposing an explanation of the twenty-first psalm, at the beginning of which is written what the Lord cried out on the cross, because that friend asked me to explain it first), I resolved all five matters—not in the order in which they had been asked but as they could be dealt with appropriately, each in its own place, in the course of my discussion of the grace of the New Testament.

This book begins in this way: "You asked me to discuss five questions."

---

141. This appears among Augustine's works as Letter 140 and was probably written in 412. Honoratus was a catechumen in Carthage, and he is sometimes identified with the Honoratus for whom Augustine wrote *The Advantage of Believing* some twenty years previously. See *Revisions* I,14.
142. See Mt 25:1-13.
143. See Mt 22:13.
144. "Recent heresy": see p. 45, n. 104.

37 (64). One Book For Marcellinus On The Spirit And The Letter
(De Spiritu Et Littera Ad Marcellinum Liber Unus)[145]

The person for whom I wrote three books entitled *The Punishment and Remission of Sins*,[146] in which there is also a detailed discussion of the baptism of infants,[147] wrote back to me that he was greatly disturbed because I said that it is possible for a person to be sinless if his will does not lack the ability, thanks to divine assistance, although no one has been, or is, or will be so perfectly righteous in this life.[148] He asked how I said that this could be the case when there is no precedent for it. Because of this questioning of his I wrote the book whose title is *The Spirit and the Letter*, in which I studied the apostolic words that say, *The letter kills, but the spirit gives life* (2 Cor 3:6). In this book, as much as God gave me help, I argued forcefully against the enemies of God's grace, whereby the wicked person is made righteous.

But when I was treating of the observances of the Jews, who in keeping with the old law abstain from certain foods, I spoke of the ceremonies of certain foods,[149] which is a term that is not used in the sacred writings. Yet it seemed appropriate to me because I remembered that "ceremonies," as though the word were *carimoniae*, comes from *carere*,[150] since those who observe them lack the things from which they are abstaining. If there is another origin of this word that is antithetical to true religion, I did not speak in accordance with it but in accordance with the one that I mentioned above.

This book begins in this way: "Having read the works that I recently prepared for you, my dearest son Marcellinus."

---

145. Written between late 412 and early 413. On Marcellinus see p. 140, n. 131.
146. I.e., Marcellinus.
147. See *Revisions* II,33.
148. See *The Punishment and Remission of Sins* II,6,7-7,8.
149. 21,36.
150. See Aulus Gellius, *Noctes Atticae* IV,9,8. "Ceremonies": *cerimonias. Carere* is the Latin for "to lack."

38 (65). One Book On Faith And Works
(De Fide Et Operibus Liber Unus)[151]

In the meantime some writings were sent to me by certain brothers, who were laymen, to be sure, but schooled in the divine scriptures. These [writings] distinguished the Christian faith from good works in such a way as to insist that without the former one could not attain to eternal life, whereas without the latter one could. In response to them I wrote a book whose title is *Faith and Works*. In it I discussed not only how those who have been regenerated by the grace of Christ ought to live but also what sort of people should be admitted to the bath of regeneration.[152]

This book begins in this way: "It seems to some people."

39 (66). A Summary Of The Conference With The Donatists, In Three Books
(Breviculus Collationis Cum Donatistis, Libri Tres)[153]

After our conference with the Donatists took place, I recalled briefly the events that occurred, and I put them in writing, keeping to the sequence of the three days that we met with them. I considered this a useful work for any well-informed person, so that he could have easy access to what happened or, after consulting the numbers that I assigned to particular topics, could read whatever he wished in the same proceedings at the relevant place, because such things weary a reader when they are too lengthy. The title of this work is *A Summary of the Conference*.

This work begins in this way: "When the Catholic bishops and those of the party of Donatus."

---

151. Written in 413.
152. See Ti 3:5.
153. The conference in question was the historic Conference of Carthage, held in Carthage in early June 411 to resolve the century-old dispute between the Catholics and the Donatists. At the conclusion of the conference Marcellinus (see p. 140, n. 131), who had been assigned as its president by the emperor, declared that the Catholics had won the debate. This is often said to mark the beginning of Donatism's slow decline.

40 (67). ONE BOOK IN ANSWER TO THE DONATISTS
AFTER THE CONFERENCE
(Post Collationem Contra Donatistas Liber Unus)[154]

I also wrote a long and I think sufficiently detailed book for the Donatists after the conference that we had with their bishops,[155] so that they would not be led further astray by them. In it I also responded to certain falsehoods of theirs that came to our attention and that, even after they had been vanquished, they tossed about where they could and as they could, in addition to what I said about the events of the conference, from which one could learn quickly what took place. I did this much more briefly in a letter again addressed to the same persons, but, because everyone who was at the council of Numidia wanted it to be taken care of there, it is not among my letters. It begins in this way: "Silvanus the primate, Valentinus, Innocent, Maximinus, Optatus, Augustine, Donatus and the other bishops of the Council of Zerta to the Donatists."[156]

This book begins in this way: "Why, O Donatists, are you still being led astray?"

41 (68). ONE BOOK ON SEEING GOD
(De Videndo Deo Liber Unus)[157]

I wrote a book on seeing God, in which I postponed a more detailed investigation about the spiritual body that will exist in the resurrection of the saints, as to whether or how *God, who is spirit* (Jn 4:24), may be seen by a body like that. But later, and to my own satisfaction, I resolved that question, which is indeed very difficult, in the last—that is, the twenty-second—book of

---

154. Written in the second half of 412.
155. I.e., the Conference of Carthage. See p. 145, n. 153.
156. Letter 141. The Council of Zerta in Numidia was held on June 14, 412.
157. Included among Augustine's letters as Letter 147, written in 413 or 414 and addressed to Paulina, an African Catholic laywoman.

The City of God.[158] I also found in a certain codex of ours, in which this book also exists, a certain memorandum on this subject which was composed by me and addressed to Fortunatianus, the bishop of Sicca.[159] It is listed in the index of my works neither among my books nor among my letters.[160]

This book begins in this way: "Recalling the debt."

The other item [i.e., the memorandum] begins: "As I asked when present and now remind."

42 (69). One Book On Nature And Grace
(De Natura Et Gratia Liber Unus)[161]

At the time there also came into my hands a certain book of Pelagius. In it, by whatever arguments he could, he defended the nature of man against the grace of God whereby the wicked person is made righteous and we are Christians. And so in this book, which I called *Nature and Grace*, I responded to this by defending grace not as something that is against nature but as something by which nature is liberated and governed.

In it I defended certain phrases that Pelagius quoted[162] that seemed to be from Sixtus, the Roman bishop and martyr, as though they were actually from that same Sixtus, for that was what I thought. But afterwards I read that they were from Sextus the philosopher and not Sixtus the Christian.[163]

This book begins in this way: "The book that you sent."

---

158. See *The City of God* XXII,29.
159. Fortunatianus was the Catholic bishop of Sicca Veneria and a major figure at the Council of Carthage in 411 (see p. 145, n. 153).
160. The memorandum seems to have been lost.
161. Written in 415. See also *Revisions* I, 9, 3 and p. 47, n. 120.
162. 64,77. The sense of this is that Pelagius cited Sixtus in favor of his own doctrine of free will, while Augustine says that he is misinterpreting Sixtus.
163. Sixtus (or Xystus) was bishop of Rome from 257 to 258. A certain Sextus, a Pythagorean philosopher, was the supposed author or compiler of a book of *Sentences*, still extant, that could easily be understood from a Christian perspective. The two were often either identified or confused with one another in Christian antiquity, and whether they were separate individuals or the same person is still disputed.

43 (70). Twenty-Two Books On The City Of God
(De Civitate Dei Libri Viginti Duo)[164]

1. In the meantime Rome was devastated by an assault on the part of the Goths acting under King Alaric and by a most destructive invasion.[165] Worshipers of the many false gods, whom we usually call pagans, attempted to impute the devastation to the Christian religion and began to blaspheme against the true God with more harshness and bitterness than usual. Hence, burning with zeal for the house of God,[166] I started to write the books *On the City of God* in answer to their blasphemies and errors. This work occupied me for a number of years, because many other matters interfered that it would not have been right to put off, and I had to use my time to address them first. But finally this vast work *On the City of God*, in twenty-two books, was finished.

Of these, the first five refute those who want human affairs to prosper and who therefore think it necessary for this to worship the many gods that the pagans are accustomed to worship, and who contend that these evils arise and abound because this is forbidden.

The following five respond to those who acknowledge that these evils have never been wanting, nor ever will be, as far as human beings are concerned, and who say that they are sometimes great and sometimes small, depending on places, times and persons, but who argue that the worship of many gods, which involves sacrificing to them, is useful in view of the life that will exist after death.

With these ten books, then, those two vain opinions that are inimical to the Christian religion are refuted.

2. But lest anyone blame us for having only disproved what other people say and for not having explained our [teachings],

---

164. Begun around 412 and completed between 426 and 427.
165. This is dated to August 410.
166. See Ps 69:9; Jn 2:17.

there is another part to this work which is devoted to that purpose and which is comprised of twelve books, although when necessary we also explain what is ours in the ten earlier [books] and disprove what is opposed to that in the twelve later ones.

Of the next twelve books, then, the first four deal with the origin of the two cities, of which one is God's and the other is this world's; the second four with their development or trajectory; and the third four, which are the last, with their merited ends.

And so, although all twenty-two books were written about both cities, they nonetheless took their title from the better one, so that it is called *The City of God.*

In the tenth of these books, the flame produced from heaven that ran between the divided victims in Abraham's sacrifice[167] ought not to have been characterized as a miracle,[168] because this was shown to him in a vision.

In the seventeenth, what was said of Samuel, "He was not from the sons of Aaron,"[169] should instead have been "He was not the son of a priest." It was a more legitimate custom, in fact, for the sons of priests to succeed the dead priests. For Samuel's father is numbered among the sons of Aaron,[170] but he was not a priest, nor is he [listed] among Aaron's sons as though he himself had begotten him, but he was like all of that people, who are called sons of Israel.

This work begins in this way: "The most glorious city of God."

---

167. See Gn 15:17.
168. X,8.
169. XVII,5.
170. There is no reference to this in scripture. See also *Revisions* II,55,2.

44 (71). One Book For The Presbyter Orosius In Refutation Of The Priscillianists And The Origenists

(Ad Orosium Presbyterum Contra Priscillianistas Et Origenistas Liber Unus)[171]

Meanwhile I responded with as much brevity and clarity as I could to the inquiry of a certain Orosius, a Spanish presbyter, about the Priscillianists and about certain opinions of Origen that the Catholic faith rejects. The title of this work is *For Orosius in Refutation of the Priscillianists and the Origenists*. The inquiry itself was added to my response at the beginning.

This book begins in this way: "To respond to your question, my dearest son Orosius."

45 (72). Two Books For The Presbyter Jerome, One On The Origin Of The Soul And The Other On A Phrase Of James

(Ad Hieronimum Presbyterum Libri Duo, Unus De Origine Animae Et Alius De Sententia Iacobi)[172]

I also wrote two books for the presbyter Jerome, who was living in Bethlehem. One was on the origin of man's soul and the other on a phrase of the apostle James, where he says, *Whoever observes the whole law but goes against it in one part has become guilty of all of it* (Jas 2:10), and in each instance I sought his advice. I did not resolve the first question that I posed. As far as

---

171. Written in 415. Orosius, born in either present-day Portugal or Spain in the last quarter of the fourth century, had met Augustine in Hippo in 414. Subsequently he provided Augustine with information about both the Priscillianists and the Origenists and asked him to refute them. Orosius's most well-known writing is the *Seven Books of History against the Pagans*, which he claimed to have composed at Augustine's request.
  The Priscillianists were so called after Priscillian, a Spanish layman who flourished in the late fourth century and who seems to have taught gnostic and ascetic doctrines. The Origenists took their name from Origen, the Alexandrian theologian who died c. 254; their teachings were loosely based on what they knew of his.
172. Written in 415 and included in Augustine's correspondence as Letters 166 and 167. Jerome (c. 347-c.420), the great Latin commentator on scripture and promoter of monastic life, was an occasional correspondent of Augustine's.

the second was concerned, however, I was not silent about how it seemed to me it should be resolved, but I wanted to see whether he himself would approve of it. He wrote back to me praising my inquiry, but he replied that he did not have the leisure to respond. I did not want to publish these books as long as he was in the body, in case he eventually responded, and then it would have been better for them to be published with his response. Once he had died, though, I published the first. With that the reader would be forewarned either not to ask at all how the soul is given to those who are born or at least to allow for a resolution of this question on an obscure matter that would not be contrary to the most evident facts that the Catholic faith knows concerning original sin in infants—that, unless they are regenerated in Christ, they will certainly be condemned.[173] But [I published] the second so that what seemed to us to be the answer to the question concerning what is mentioned there would be made known.

This work begins in this way: "Our God, who has called us."

46 (73). ONE BOOK FOR EMERITUS, A BISHOP OF THE DONATISTS, AFTER THE CONFERENCE
(Ad Emeritum Episcopum Donatistarum Post Collationem Liber Unus)[174]

Sometime after the conference of ours that we held with them, I wrote a book addressed to Emeritus, a bishop of the Donatists, who was seen to defend their cause mightily at that same conference. The book is quite useful because it includes with suitable brevity the facts whereby they are defeated or are shown to have been defeated.

This book begins in this way: "If even now, brother Emeritus."

---

173. On the origin of the soul see p. 28, n. 20.
174. This work, which is lost, was probably written soon after the Conference of Carthage in 411 (see p. 145, n. 153), although its place in the *Revisions* suggests that it may have been written several years after that. Emeritus was the Donatist bishop of Caesarea, the capital of Mauretania Caesariensis, and he played a significant role at the conference. He is also the subject of *The Proceedings with Emeritus*. See *Revisions* II,51.

47 (74). One Book On The Deeds Of Pelagius
(De Gestis Pelagii Liber Unus)[175]

During the same time in the Orient—that is, in Syria Palaestina—Pelagius was brought by some Catholic brothers to an assembly of bishops.[176] Those who had brought the accusation against him were absent,[177] because they were unable to appear on the day of the synod, but he was heard by fourteen bishops. At it they pronounced him Catholic when he condemned those teachings that are inimical to the grace of Christ and that were read out to him from the accusation. But when those same acts came into our hands, I wrote a book about them lest, when he was seemingly acquitted, the judges would also be thought to have approved those same teachings. And, had he not condemned them, he would never have left them [i.e., the judges] without having been condemned.

This book begins in this way: "After [there came] into our hands."

48 (75). One Book On The Correction
Of The Donatists
(De Correctione Donatistarum Liber Unus)[178]

At the same time I also wrote a book on the correction of the Donatists because of those who did not want them to be corrected by the imperial laws.

This book begins in this way: "I praise and congratulate and admire."

---

175. Written about 416.
176. This was the Synod of Diospolis (Lydda, in present-day Israel), held in late 415.
177. I.e., the Catholic brothers, who were two bishops from Gaul.
178. This appears in Augustine's correspondence as Letter 185, written in 417 to the Roman official Boniface.

49 (76). One Book For Dardanus
On The Presence Of God
(De Praesentia Dei Ad Dardanum Liber Unus)[179]

I wrote a book on the presence of God, in which we devoted our attention especially to the Pelagian heresy, which was not mentioned by name. In it there is also a careful and detailed discussion of the presence of the nature that we call the most high and true God, and likewise of his temple.

This book begins in this way: "I acknowledge, my dearest brother Dardanus."

50 (77). Two Books For Albina, Pinianus And Melania,
In Answer To Pelagius And Caelestius,
On The Grace Of Christ And Original Sin
(Contra Pelagium Et Caelestium De Gratia Christi
Et De Peccato Originali Ad Albinam,
Pinianum Et Melaniam Libri Duo)[180]

After the Pelagian heresy, along with its originators, was shown to be erroneous and was condemned by the bishops of Rome, first by Innocent and then by Zosimus,[181] with the aid of documentation from African councils,[182] I wrote two books against them, one on the grace of Christ and the other on original sin.

This work begins in this way: "How greatly we rejoice at your bodily and especially your spiritual health."

---

179. This appears in Augustine's correspondence as Letter 187, addressed to Claudius Postumus Dardanus, a distinguished Catholic layman in Italy, and written in mid-417.
180. Written in 418 in response to a letter from Albina, Pinianus and Melania, which is now lost. The three addressees were wealthy members of the Roman nobility and figure in Letters 124-126. Pinianus and Melania were married, and Albina was Melania's mother. They were drawn to the ascetic life and were friends of Pelagius, who was a promoter of asceticism.
181. Innocent was bishop of Rome from 401 to 417, Zosimus from 417 to 418. Innocent excommunicated Pelagius and Caelestius in 417. Zosimus initially acquitted Pelagius and seemed ready to acquit Caelestius as well, but for reasons that are not entirely clear he changed his mind and condemned Pelagianism.
182. The councils in question would certainly be those of Carthage (416), Milevis (416) and Carthage again (418).

51 (78). The Proceedings With Emeritus, A Bishop Of The Donatists, In One Book

(Gesta Cum Emerito Donatistarum Episcopo Liber Unus)[183]

Sometime after the conference that we held with the Donatist heretics, the need arose for us to travel to Mauritania Caesarea. There in Caesarea itself we saw Emeritus, the bishop of the Donatists, who was one of the seven whom they had delegated to defend their cause and who had labored mightily on behalf of that same cause.[184] The ecclesiastical acts (which are recorded in my works) document our debate with him in the presence of the bishops of the same province and of the people of the church of Caesarea, in which city he was both a citizen and the bishop of the aforementioned heretics. When he could come up with no response, he listened as though mute to my entire speech, which was an explanation solely of the Maximianists[185] that was intended for his ears and those of all who were present.

This book or rather these proceedings begin in this way: "When the most glorious Honorius, consul for the twelfth time, and Theodosius, consul for the eighth time, were emperors, on the twelfth day before the Kalends of October at Caesarea in the greater church."

52 (79). One Book In Answer To A Sermon Of The Arians

(Contra Sermonem Arianorum Liber Unus)[186]

During this time there fell into my hands a certain anonymous sermon of the Arians. At the insistent request of the person who had sent it to me,[187] I responded to it as briefly and as rapidly as

---

183. Composed in 418. The opening words of the work indicate that the proceedings took place on September 20, 418. On Emeritus see also *Revisions* II,46 and p. 151, n. 174.
184. The seven were, in addition to Emeritus, Primian, Petilian, Protasius, Montanus, Gaudentius and Adeodatus. See *The Acts of the Conference of Carthage* I,148.
185. On the Maximianists see p. 134, nn. 107 and 108.
186. Written in 418 or 419.
187. This person may have been Dionysius of Vicus Juliani, a town located near Hippo. See Letter 23A*,3.

I could. With the same sermon added at the beginning of my response, and thanks to the use of numbers that indicate which passage I am responding to, it is easy to read.

This book (after their sermon, which was added at the beginning) begins in this way: "With this argument I am responding to their preceding argument."

53 (80). Two Books On Marriage And Desire For Valerius
(De Nuptiis Et Concupiscentia Ad Valerium Libri Duo)[188]

I wrote two books for the illustrious man, Count Valerius, when I heard that the Pelagians had written something or other to him about us—namely, that by affirming original sin we were condemning marriage. The title of these books is *Marriage and Desire*. Of course we defended the goodness of marriage, lest it be thought that the desire of the flesh and the law in our members opposing the law of our mind[189] was a vice associated with it, since conjugal chastity makes good use of this evil of sexual desire for the procreation of children. The reason for two books is that the first fell into the hands of the Pelagian Julian, and he wrote four books in response to it,[190] from which someone collected excerpts

---

188. The first book was written in 418-419, the second in 420 or 421. Valerius was a Catholic layman and an important figure in the imperial court at Ravenna. He had been appealed to by Julian of Eclanum, a leading proponent of Pelagianism (see n. 190 below), after he had been condemned by Pope Zosimus in 418 for refusing to subscribe to an anti-Pelagian statement authored by the pope. When asking for redress from Valerius, Julian also complained to him that Augustine had demeaned marriage. Augustine's Letter 200 reveals that there was some correspondence, now lost, on this issue between Valerius and himself. *Marriage and Desire* is Augustine's attempt to respond to Julian's accusation, which Julian expanded upon after the first book of *Marriage and Desire* had been composed and he had had a chance to read it, which necessitated the second book. This treatise is the first in a series of writings directed against Julian.
189. See Rom 7:23.
190. See *Unfinished Work in Answer to Julian* I,16; IV,3. The Julian is Julian of Eclanum (c. 380-c. 454), who was Augustine's chief Pelagian antagonist in his final years and the object of a number of his writings. His turbulent career was marked by several condemnations and banishments. Eclanum (or Aeclanum) was located in south-central Italy.

and sent them to Count Valerius, which he in turn sent to us. When I received them, I responded to those same issues with the second book.

The first book of this work begins in this way: "The recent heretics,[191] my dearest son Valerius."

And the second in this way: "Amid the preoccupations of your military life."

54 (81). Seven Books On Expressions In The Heptateuch
(Locutionum In Heptateuchum Libri Septem)[192]

I composed seven books on seven books of divine scripture—namely, the five of Moses, the one of Joshua, the son of Nun, and the other of the Judges—in which I noted particular expressions that are unusual from the perspective of our language. Those who read [scripture] while paying too little attention to such things seek the meaning of the divine words, although this is [merely] a kind of expression, and they occasionally extract something that is not in fact far from the truth, even though the author by whom it was written is found not to have thought that; yet, on account of the particular expression, it seems more believable that he said this. But many obscure things in the holy scriptures become clear once the particular expression is understood. For that reason those same expressions should be known where the meanings are clear, so that even where they are hidden this knowledge may assist in revealing them to the attentive reader. The title of this work is *Expressions from Genesis*, and so on for each of the books.[193]

In the first book I noted what was written, *And Noah did all the words whatsoever that the Lord commanded him to; thus did he do* (Gn 6:22; 7:5), and I said that it was an expression similar to the one that occurs in the making of the created world. After it

---

191. "The recent heretics": see p. 45, n. 104.
192. Probably written in 419 in conjunction with the following work.
193. I.e., *Expressions from Exodus*, etc.

says, *And thus it was done* (Gn 1:15.24), there is added, *And God made* (Gn 1:16.25). The one does not seem to me to be similar in every respect. In the former instance the meaning is also hidden, while in the latter it is merely an expression.

This work begins in this way: "The expressions of the scriptures."

55 (82). Seven Books Of Questions On The Heptateuch *(Quaestionum In Heptateuchum Libri Septem)*[194]

1. At the same time I also wrote books of questions on the same seven sacred books, which I wanted to refer to in that way [i.e., as questions] because the things that are discussed there I proposed as questions that I was asking rather than as questions that I had answered, although it seems to me that the majority of them were dealt with in such a way that they could not unjustifiably be considered to have been resolved and explained. We had already begun to examine the Books of Kingdoms in the same way, but we did not make much progress because we focused our attention on other things that were more urgent.

In the first book there is a discussion about the different rods that Jacob put in the water,[195] so that the sheep that were breeding would see them when they drank and would bear variegated young.[196] We did not give a good explanation for why he did not put them again before those that were breeding—that is, when they were breeding other young—but [only] when they were breeding for the first time. For the explanation of another question, when it is asked why Jacob said to his father-in-law, *You defrauded me of my salary by ten lambs* (Gn 31:41), indicates that, while it was posed accurately enough, it was not resolved as it should have been.

194. Probably written in 419.
195. I,93.
196. See Gn 30:37-39.

2. In the third book there is a discussion of the high priest and how he begot children,[197] since he was obliged to enter the Holy of Holies twice a day, where the altar of incense was located, in order to offer incense in the morning and in the evening.[198] As the law says, he could not enter it unclean, and the same law says that a man becomes unclean even through marital relations; indeed, it orders him to bathe in water, and it says that, once he has bathed, he is unclean until evening.[199] That is why I said, "It follows from this that either he was continent or that on some days he would omit the incense." I did not see that this did not follow. For what is written, *He shall be unclean until evening*, can be understood to mean that he would no longer be unclean through the evening itself but only up to it, so that already by eventide, as someone who was clean, he might offer incense, although he had had relations with his wife after the morning incense in order to beget children.[200]

Likewise, where the question is raised as to how the high priest was forbidden to attend his father's funeral,[201] since it was not permitted for him to become a priest until after the death of the priest who was his father, when there was only one [high priest], I said, "Hence his son, who would succeed his father, had to be appointed immediately after his father's death, before he was buried, for the sake of maintaining the continuity of the incense, which had to be offered twice a day."[202] As priest he was forbidden to be near the corpse of his unburied father. But I paid no attention to the possibility that this command could have been given on account of those who were going to be high priests without succeeding high priests who were their

197. III,82.85.
198. See Ex 30:7-8.
199. See Lv 15:16.
200. It is noteworthy that, although the biblical prescription says nothing about sexual relations "in order to beget children," Augustine adds this qualification as being the sole justification for blameless intercourse. See *The Excellence of Marriage* 6, 6.
201. See Lv 21:11.
202. III,83.

fathers. They would still have been from the sons—that is, from the descendents—of Aaron, even were it the case that the high priest either had no sons or had ones who were so wicked that none of them ought to have succeeded their father, which was how Samuel succeeded the high priest Eli,[203] although he himself was not the priest's son. But he was nonetheless from the sons—that is, from the descendents—of Aaron.[204]

3. With respect to the thief to whom it was said, *This day you shall be with me in paradise* (Lk 23:43), I put it down as though it were certain that he had not been visibly baptized, although that is uncertain, and instead it should be believed that he *was* baptized, as I also discussed afterwards in another place.[205]

Again, I said in the fifth book that, when mothers are mentioned in the gospel genealogies,[206] they are not listed apart from fathers.[207] This is certainly true, but it is irrelevant to the matter that was under discussion. The discussion was about those who married the wives of their brothers or close relatives who had died without offspring, and it was on account of the two fathers of Joseph, one of whom is mentioned by Matthew and the other by Luke. I discussed this matter in detail in the present work, when we were revising our work *In Answer to Faustus, a Manichean.*[208]

This work begins in this way: "Since the holy scriptures, which are called canonical."

---

203. See 1 S 2:12-4:1.
204. See *Revisions* II,43,2 and note p. 149, n. 170.
205. III,84. On the topic of the thief's baptism see also *Revisions* I,26,2, question 62; II,18.
206. See Mt 1:16; Lk 3:23.
207. V,46.
208. *Revisions* II,7,2. See also II,12;16.

56 (83). Four Books On The Soul And Its Origin
(De Anima Et Eius Origine Libri Quattuor)[209]

At the same time a certain Vincent Victor[210] in Mauretania Caesariensis[211] came upon one of my works in the possession of a certain Peter, a Spanish presbyter.[212] There was a certain passage in it on the origin of the soul of individual human beings in which I acknowledged that I did not know whether they were generated from that one [soul] of the first man and, after that, from parents, or whether, as was the case with that one man, they were bestowed on an individual basis apart from any generation,[213] but that I did know that the soul was not a body but a spirit. In response to what I said he wrote two books for that same Peter, which the monk Renatus[214] sent to me from Caesarea. When I had read them, I sent back four with my response—one for the monk Renatus, another for the presbyter Peter, and two for that same Victor. The one addressed to Peter, although it is book-length, is nonetheless a letter that I did not want to be separate from the other three. But in all of them, in which many important things are discussed, I defended my hesitation in regard to the origin of the souls that are bestowed on individual human beings, and I demonstrated the many er-

---

209. Probably written between 419 and 421.
210. Vincent Victor was a young man and a recent convert to Catholicism from Donatism; when responding to him in *The Soul and its Origin* Augustine gives a brief account of what he knows of him in III,1,1-2,2. The work by Augustine that Vincent is said to have discovered in Peter's possession seems to have been Letter 190, in which Augustine confesses ignorance about certain aspects of the soul. This admission scandalized Vincent and furnished him with the occasion to write the two books that are referred to and that are now lost; in them he espoused the notion that God directly created souls for each human being, which Augustine had said was unclear in scripture. On the issue of the origin of the soul in the *Revisions* see p. 28, n. 20.
211. Mauretania Caesariensis was a Roman province in North Africa whose chief city was Caesarea.
212. Peter is described in II,1,1 as an old man who embraced Victor's opinions; nothing more is known of him.
213. See also *Revisions* I,1,3.
214. Renatus is depicted in I,1,1-2,2 as someone who is friendly towards Augustine. Letter 23* is addressed to him.

rors and evils that result from his presumption.²¹⁵ Nevertheless I treated the young man with as much gentleness as I could, not as someone who should forthwith be disdained but as someone who was still teachable, and I accepted his corrections from him.

The book for Renatus from this work begins in this way: "Your sincerity in our regard."

That for Peter begins in this way: "To my lord and dearest brother and fellow presbyter Peter."

Of the two final [books] for Vincent Victor the first begins in this way: "That I thought that I should write to you."

57 (84). Two Books For Pollentius On Adulterous Marriages
*(Ad Pollentium De Adulterinis Coniugiis Libri Duo)*²¹⁶

I wrote two books on adulterous marriages, following the scriptures as closely as possible, with the intention of solving a very difficult problem.²¹⁷ I do not know whether I was able to do this in a very clear way. Indeed, I do not think that I concluded the matter, although I shed light on many of its obscurities. An intelligent reader will be able to judge it.

The first book of this work begins in this way: "The first question, dearest brother Pollentius, is."

The second begins in this way: "In response to what you wrote to me."

---

215. I.e., that of Victor, who presumed to find in scripture what Augustine insisted could not be found there.
216. Written between late 419 and early 420. Pollentius, who is otherwise unknown, had written twice to Augustine on marriage and especially on the possibility of divorce from a scriptural standpoint.
217. I.e., whether the New Testament allows for divorce under some circumstances.

58 (85). Two Books In Answer To An Adversary Of The Law And The Prophets
(Contra Adversarium Legis Et Prophetarum Libri Duo)[218]

During that period a book was being read in a piazza by the sea in Carthage, where many people converged and listened very attentively. It was by a certain heretic, either a Marcionite[219] or one of those whose erroneous opinion is that God did not make this world and that the God of the law that was given through Moses, and of the prophets who belong to that same law, is not the true God but a most evil demon. There were Christian brothers who, in their great zeal, obtained it [i.e., the book] and sent it to me to be refuted without delay; they asked persistently that I not put off giving a response. I proved it wrong in two books, which I entitled *An Answer to an Adversary of the Law and the Prophets*, because the codex itself that had been sent did not include the author's name.

This work begins in this way: "To the book that you sent, dearest brothers."

59 (86). Two Books In Answer To Gaudentius, A Bishop Of The Donatists
(Contra Gaudentium Donatistarum Episcopum Libri Duo)[220]

At the same time the tribune and notary Dulcitius was here in Africa to execute the imperial orders that had been given against the Donatists.[221] He had sent a letter to Gaudentius of Thamugadi, a bishop of the Donatists and one of those seven whom they had chosen to speak in their defense at our conference,[222] in which he urged him to Catholic unity and tried to prevent the fire with which he

---

218. Written between 418 and 423.
219. Marcion, who died c. 160, posited a harsh God of the Old Testament and a merciful God of the New, who was the father of Christ.
220. Probably written in 420.
221. This is the same Dulcitius at whose request *The Eight Questions of Dulcitius* was written. He was the brother of Laurence, for whom Augustine wrote *Faith, Hope and Charity*.
222. This was the Conference of Carthage, held in 411 (see p. 145, n. 153). The seven bishops are named at p. 154, n. 184.

threatened to destroy himself and his followers along with the very church that he was in. He also added that, if they considered themselves in the right, they ought rather to flee in accordance with the command of the Lord Christ[223] than to burn themselves up in wicked flames. He [i.e., Gaudentius] replied with two letters; one of them was brief because the messenger was in a hurry, as he noted, while the other was lengthy, as though offering a fuller and more careful response. The aforementioned tribune thought that these should be sent to me, so that I myself might refute them instead. I showed in a single book that both were erroneous. When this [book] came into the hands of the same Gaudentius, he wrote back to me what he thought, providing no rationale in his response but instead declaring that he was incapable of either responding or keeping silent. Although this might have been enough for intelligent readers who compare our writings with his, I still did not want to leave whatever it was [that he wrote] without a response. That is how it turned out that these two books of ours were addressed to him.

This work begins in this way: "Gaudentius, bishop of the Donatists of Thamugadi."

60 (87). ONE BOOK AGAINST LYING
(Contra Mendacium Liber Unus)[224]

At the time I also wrote a book against lying. The reason for this work was that, in order to investigate the Priscillianist heretics,[225] who think that their heresy must be kept hidden not only by denial and lying[226] but even by committing perjury, it seemed to certain Catholics that they should feign being Priscillianists in order to penetrate their hiding-places. I authored this book, forbidding their doing this.

This book begins in this way: "You have sent me many things to read."

---

223. See Mt 10:23.
224. Written about 420.
225. On the Priscillianists see p. 150, n. 171.
226. See 11,25; 21,41.

61 (88). Four Books In Answer To Two Letters Of The Pelagians
(Contra Duas Epistolas Pelagianorum Libri Quattuor)[227]

There follow four books that I wrote for Bishop Boniface of the Roman church[228] in answer to two letters of the Pelagians, because, when they came into his hands, he sent them to me, having discovered my name mentioned in them with injurious intent.

This work begins in this way: "I have indeed known you, thanks to your widespread reputation."

62 (89). Six Books In Answer To Julian
(Contra Iulianum Libri Sex)[229]

Meanwhile four books by the Pelagian Julian, which I mentioned above, also came into my hands. In them I learned that what had been excerpted from them by the person who had sent them to Count Valerius[230] was not exactly what was said by Julian and addressed to the same count; instead, parts of it had been somewhat changed. I therefore wrote six books in answer to those four. The first two of mine refute Julian's impudence with the testimonies of the saints who defended the Catholic faith after the time of the apostles. He thought that we ought to be reproached as though our teaching were Manichean, because we say that it is from Adam that original sin is derived, which is washed away in the bath of regeneration[231] not only in the case of adults but also in that of infants. But how much assistance Julian himself offers the Manicheans in several opinions of his I demonstrated

---

227. Written about 420. One of the two letters was written by Julian of Eclanum (see p. 155, nn. 188 and 190) to the Pelagians in Rome, and the other by a group of Pelagian bishops to Bishop Rufus of Thessalonica; each is extensively cited in Augustine's treatise.
228. Boniface was bishop of Rome from 418 to 422.
229. Written in 421 or shortly after. This was Julian of Eclanum.
230. Valerius was a Count of Africa in the early fifth century who, by the time *The Answer to Julian* was written, was at the imperial court in Ravenna. He was a devout Catholic and an occasional correspondent of Augustine.
231. See Tit 3:5.

in the final part of my first book. The other four [books] of ours, however, respond to each of his on an individual basis.

In the fifth volume of this lengthy and detailed work, though, where I mentioned a deformed married man who was accustomed to placing a beautiful picture in front of his wife when they were having sexual relations, lest he beget deformed children,[232] I put down the name of the man who was accustomed to doing this as if I were sure of it, although I am unsure of it because my memory has failed me. In any event Soranus, a medical author, wrote that a Cypriot king was in the habit of doing this, but he did not mention his proper name.[233]

This work begins in this way: "Your abusive and slanderous words, Julian."

63 (90). One Book For Laurence On Faith, Hope And Charity
(Ad Laurentium De Fide, Spe Et Caritate Liber Unus)[234]

I also wrote a book on faith, hope and charity when the person for whom it was written asked me if he might have some small work of mine that would not leave his hands—the kind that the Greeks call an *enchiridion*.[235] It seems to me that in it I summarized with sufficient care how God should be worshiped, which divine scripture very correctly defines as man's true wisdom.[236]

This book begins in this way: "I cannot say, my dearest son Laurence, how delighted I am by your learning."

---

232. V,14,51.
233. See Soranus of Ephesus, *Gynaecia* I,39,1. Soranus lived in the second half of the first and the first half of the second centuries AD and was a reputable medical authority in antiquity, known particularly for a four-volume work on gynecology. His writings are used, without always being acknowledged, by several early Christian writers.
234. Probably written during the period 419-422. Laurence was a learned layman and the brother of the Dulcitius for whom Augustine compiled *The Eight Questions of Dulcitius*.
235. From Greek words meaning "in the hand." This work of Augustine's is in fact more commonly referred to as *The Enchiridion*.
236. 2,1.

64 (91). One Book For Bishop Paulinus On The Care To Be Taken Of The Dead
(De Cura Pro Mortuis Gerenda Ad Paulinum Episcopum Liber Unus)[237]

I wrote a book on the care to be taken of the dead when I had been asked in a letter whether it is of value to someone if, after his death, his body is buried near the memorial of some saint.

This book begins in this way: "For a long time, my venerable brother bishop Paulinus, [I have owed] Your Holiness."

65 (92). One Book On The Eight Questions Of Dulcitius
(De Octo Dulcitii Quaestionibus Liber Unus)[238]

The book that I entitled *The Eight Questions of Dulcitius* should not have been listed among my books in this work, since it was put together from items that were previously written by me elsewhere, except that there is also part of a discussion that we included in it, and to one of the questions I gave a response that was not from another work of mine but that occurred to me at the time.

This book begins in this way: "As much as seems to me, my dearest son Dulcitius."

---

237. Written about 422. Paulinus (c. 355-431) was bishop of Nola in Italy and an occasional correspondent of Augustine's. He was responsible for the tomb of the martyr Felix of Nola, and he had written to Augustine to ask him about the value of being buried near the grave of Felix (or any other saint); that letter is lost.
238. Composed about 425. On Dulcitius see *Revisions* II, 59 and p. 162, n. 222.

66 (93). One Book For Valentine And The Monks With Him On Grace And Free Choice

(Ad Valentinum Et Cum Illo Monachos De Gratia Et Libero Arbitrio Unus Liber)[239]

For the sake of those who, when the grace of God is being defended, think that free choice is being denied, and who defend free choice in such a way as to deny God's grace, declaring that it is given in accordance with our merits, I wrote a book whose title is *Grace and Free Choice*. I wrote it for the monks of Hadrumetum. Such contention had arisen in their monastery about this matter that some of them were compelled to ask my opinion.

This book begins in this way: "For the sake of those who [proclaim and defend] the free choice of man."

67 (94). One Book For The Aforementioned On Rebuke And Grace

(Ad Quos Supra De Correptione Et Gratia Liber Unus)[240]

I wrote another book again for the same persons that I called *Rebuke and Grace*, when I was told that someone there had said that no one ought to be rebuked if he does not carry out God's commands; instead, he should only be prayed for, so that he would carry them out.

This book begins in this way: "After having read your letter, my dearest brother Valentine."

---

239. Probably written soon after Easter 426. Valentine was the abbot of a monastery in Hadrumetum, in the Roman province of Byzacena in North Africa. He and Augustine had a brief correspondence on the issue discussed in this and the following treatise, of which only Augustine's letters have survived.
240. Probably written in 427. Augustine's first book for the monks at Hadrumetum had not satisfied one of the monks there, who drew an unintended conclusion from Augustine's teaching that both willing and doing were entirely gifts of God; if that were so, he maintained, no one should be rebuked for not acting rightly but should only be prayed for. Hence Augustine wrote a second book to address that problem.

Epilogue

When I revised these works, not knowing whether I was going to compose still more, I observed that I had composed ninety-three in two hundred and thirty-two books.[241] And, at the urging of the brothers, I have published the revision of them in two books, before beginning to revise my letters and my sermons to the people, some of which were written while others were spoken by me.

---

241. The number of titles is actually ninety-four; perhaps Augustine has omitted the books on the disciplines (I,6). The *Revisions* itself is of course not included. As far as books are concerned, the number comes to 254, exclusive of the books on the disciplines, and not 232. What can account for the difference of twenty-two?

Appendix I
The Indiculus of Possidius[1]

[I.] In Answer To The Pagans

1. Three books on the Academics.[2]
2. Two books on order.[3]
3. One book on the immortality of the soul.[4]
4. One book on the advantage of believing.[5]
5. One book on true religion.[6]
6. A question as to whether the soul exists of itself.[7]
7. Another as to whether it is by God's causality that humankind is evil.[8]
8. Again, another as to whether truth can be grasped by the body's senses.[9]
9. Again, another as to why Christ was born of a woman.[10]
10. Again, another on the Son.[11]
11. Again, another on God and creation.[12]
12. Again, another on the Father and the Son.[13]
13. Again, another on providence.[14]
14. Again, another on why God willed to make the world.[15]
15. Again, another on whether anything is above or below in the universe.[16]

---

1. The attribution of the listed works with known writings of Augustine is often conjectural; this is especially the case with the letters, but occasionally also with the sermons. When several letters are listed for the same person, they are footnoted in the order of their classical enumeration, with the Divjak (*) letters last. When Possidius's reference to one or more sermons could apply to yet more sermons, all of those sermons are footnoted together.
2. See *Revisions* I,1.
3. See ibid. I,3.
4. See ibid. I,5.
5. See ibid. 1,14.
6. See ibid. I,13.
7. *A Miscellany of Eighty-three Questions* 1. (For all references to *A Miscellany of Eight-three Questions* see *Revisions* I,26,2.)
8. Ibid. 3.
9. Ibid. 9.
10. Ibid. 11.
11. Ibid. 16.
12. Ibid. 19.
13. Ibid. 23.
14. Ibid. 27.
15. Ibid. 28.
16. Ibid. 29.

16. Again, another on whether one person understands something better than another person, and whether the understanding of that thing can thus proceed to infinity.[17]

17. Again, another on how the Lord Jesus Christ, who is the wisdom of God,[18] was both in his mother's womb and in heaven.[19]

18. Again, another on why the Lord Jesus Christ came after such a long time.[20]

19. Again, another on believable things.[21]

20. Four books on the agreement among the evangelists.[22]

21. Six questions explained in answer to Porphyry—namely, on the resurrection; on the time of the Christian religion; on the difference among sacrifices; on what the Lord says, *In the measure that you have measured out it will be measured back to you* (Mt 7:2); on the Son of God according to Solomon; on the prophet Jonah.[23]

22. One book on demonic divination.[24]

23. Twenty-two books on the city of God.[25]

Letters In Answer To The Aforementioned

24. To Maximus of Madaura.[26]

25. To the brothers at Carthage.

26. To the people of Madaura.[27]

27. To Dioscorus.[28]

28. To Volusian.[29]

29. To Marcellinus.[30]

30. To Macedonius, on intercessions by bishops.[31]

---

17. Ibid. 32.
18. See 1 Cor 1:24.
19. *A Miscellany of Eighty-three Questions* 42.
20. Ibid. 44.
21. Ibid. 48.
22. See *Revisions* II,16.
23. See ibid. II,31.
24. See ibid. II,30.
25. See ibid. II,43.
26. Letter 17.
27. Letter 232.
28. Letter 118.
29. Letter 137.
30. Letter 138.
31. Letter 153.

31. Again, to the same person, on the true virtues.[32]
32. Two to Longinianus.[33]

Sermons Against The Aforementioned

33. An exhortation to faith.
34. On the fear of God.[34]
35. On the Parentalia.
36. On an eclipse of the sun.
37. On Epiphany in answer to the aforementioned.
38. Again, two on Epiphany.
39. On the Kalends of January in answer to the aforementioned.
40. Two sermons on the resurrection.
41. On the reading from the Acts of the Apostles in which the Epicurean and Stoic philosophers engaged in discussion with the apostle Paul.[35]
42. On testimonies from the scriptures against the Donatists and idols.[36]

[II.] In Answer To The Mathematicians[37]

1. A question against the aforementioned.[38]
2. A letter to Lampadius.[39]

[III.] In Answer To The Jews

1. A question on the Jews.[40]
2. Again, another on the forty-six years of the building of the Temple.[41]
3. A letter to Bishop Asellicus on bewaring of the Jews.[42]
4. Two sermons against the aforementioned.

---

32. Letter 155.
33. Letters 233 and 235.
34. Sermons 347-348.
35. See Acts 17:16-34. Sermon 150.
36. Sermon 360A.
37. Astrologers were commonly referred to as mathematicians.
38. *A Miscellany of Eighty-three Questions* 45.
39. Letter 246.
40. There is no question in *A Miscellany of Eighty-three Questions*, from which Possidius draws so much of his information here, that is simply "on the Jews," although several questions deal with Old Testament, and hence Jewish, themes. Question 46, however, is entitled *De ideis* ("On ideas"), and it is conceivable that Possidius misread it as *De iudaeis* ("On the Jews"), especially since the *Indiculus* includes no entry "on ideas."
41. *A Miscellany of Eighty-three Questions* 56.
42. Letter 196.

[IV.] IN ANSWER TO THE MANICHEANS

1.   Two books on the Catholic way of life and their way of life.[43]
2.   One book on the two souls.[44]
3.   Three books on the origin of evil and on free choice.[45]
4.   The acts of a debate with Fortunatus, a Manichean, one book.[46]
5.   Two books on Genesis in answer to the Manicheans.[47]
6.   One book in answer to the letter of *The Foundation*.[48]
7.   Diverse questions, twenty-eight in number, in answer to the slanders of Adimantus.[49]
8.   A question on free choice.[50]
9.   Again, on evil.[51]
10. Another, on whether the body is from God.[52]
11. Again, another: that the body of our Lord Jesus Christ was not a phantom.[53]
12. Another, whether God is not the creator of evil.[54]
13. Again, another: God is not subject to necessity.[55]
14. Another, on whether both committing sin and acting uprightly fall under the will's free choice; that this is the case is entirely true.[56]
15. Again, another on the cross of Christ.[57]
16. Another: where do different wills of human beings come from, since souls have one nature?[58]
17. Again, another: why did the Son of God appear in a man and the Holy Spirit in a dove?[59]

---

43. See *Revisions* I,7.
44. See ibid. I,15.
45. See ibid. I,9.
46. See ibid. I,16.
47. See ibid. I,10.
48. See ibid. II,2.
49. See ibid. I,22.
50. *A Miscellany of Eighty-three Questions* 2.
51. Ibid. 6.
52. Ibid. 10.
53. Ibid. 14.
54. Ibid. 21.
55. Ibid. 22.
56. Ibid. 24.
57. Ibid. 25.
58. Ibid. 40.
59. Ibid. 43.

18. Again, another: why did the children of Israel sacrifice obla-
    tions[60] of cattle in visible fashion?[61]
19. Another, on man as made to the image and likeness of God.[62]
20. Again, another on what is said: *I regret having made man* (Gn 6:7).[63]
21. Again, another on the gold and silver that the Israelites took from
    the Egyptians.[64]
22. Again, another on what is written: *There are sixty queens and eighty
    concubines, and the young maidens are numberless* (Sg 6:8).[65]
23. Again, another on what is written: *And found in form as a man*
    (Phil 2:7).[66]
24. One book in answer to a letter of Secundinus, a Manichean.[67]
25. The acts of a debate with Felix, a Manichean, two books.[68]
26. One book on the nature of the good.[69]
27. Different questions in answer to Faustus, a Manichean, in thirty-
    three books.[70]
28. A letter to Honoratus.

SERMONS AGAINST THE AFOREMENTIONED

29. On *In the beginning God created heaven and earth* (Gn 1:1), and
    In the beginning was the Word (Jn 1:1).[71]
30. From what is written in the prophet Haggai, *Mine is the gold and
    mine is the silver* (Hg 2:8), in response to the aforementioned.[72]
31. On the Day of the Lord, according to the prophet Zephaniah,[73] in
    answer to the aforementioned.
32. From what is written in Job, *The angels came into the presence
    of God, and the devil was in their midst* (Jb 1:6), and from the

60. Reading *victimas* rather than *victimis*.
61. *A Miscellany of Eighty-three Questions* 49.
62. Ibid. 51.
63. Ibid. 52.
64. See Ex 3:22; 11:2; 12:35-36. *A Miscellany of Eighty-three Questions* 53.
65. *A Miscellany of Eighty-three Questions* 55.
66. Ibid. 73.
67. See *Revisions* II,10.
68. See ibid. II,8.
69. See ibid. II,9.
70. See ibid. II,7.
71. Sermon 1.
72. Sermon 50.
73. See Zep passim.

gospel, *Blessed are the pure of heart, for they shall see God* (Mt 5:8), in answer to the aforementioned.[74]

[V.] IN ANSWER TO THE PRISCILLIANISTS

1.   One book for [the presbyter] Orosius.[75]
2.   Two letters for Bishop Optatus on the soul.

[VI.] AGAINST THE DONATISTS

1.   An abecedarian psalm.[76]
2.   One book in answer to a letter of the heretic Donatus.[77]
3.   Two books in answer to the aforementioned.[78]
4.   Three books in answer to the letter of Parmenian.[79]
5.   Seven books on baptism in answer to the aforementioned.[80]
6.   One book in answer to a part of a letter of Petilian.[81]
7.   Again, one book in answer to the full letter of the same person.[82]
8.   One book in answer to a second letter of the same person.[83]
9.   One book in answer to a letter of Vincent, a Donatist and Rogatist.[84]
10.   One book in answer to a certain despiser sent by the aforementioned.
11.   Four books in answer to a letter of Cresconius, a grammarian.[85]
12.   One book in answer to what Centurius presented from the aforementioned.[86]
13.   One book for Constantine on the one baptism in answer to Petilianus.[87]
14.   Three books on the Maximianists in answer to the aforementioned.[88]

---

74. Sermon 12.
75. See *Revisions* II,44.
76. See ibid. I,20.
77. See ibid. I,21.
78. See ibid. II,5.
79. See ibid. II,17.
80. See ibid. II,18.
81. See ibid., II,25, book I.
82. See ibid., book II.
83. See ibid., book III.
84. Letter 93. Rogatism took its name from the Donatist bishop Rogatus, who broke away from Donatism about the year 370. Vincent was the successor of Rogatus.
85. See *Revisions* II,26.
86. See ibid. II,19.
87. See ibid. II,25.
88. Two separate works on the Maximiantists exist, but each has only one book. See ibid. II,29; 35.

15. Summaries of the acts of the conference that was held in answer to the aforementioned, three books.[89]

16. One book in answer to the aforementioned Donatists after the conference.[90]

17. One book on the correction of the Donatists.

18. One book for Emeritus, a bishop of the Donatists.[91]

19. A response in answer to two letters of Gaudentius, a bishop of the Donatists, one book.[92]

Letters In Answer To The Aforementioned

20. One book for the Catholic brothers.

21. To Januarius, the primate of the party of Donatus.[93]

22. An admonition to Primianus.

23. Two to Macrobius.[94]

24. One to Vincent.[95]

25. Four to Proculeianus.[96]

26. Two to Emeritus.[97]

27. Four to Crispinus.[98]

28. Two to Eusebius.[99]

29. Two to the people of Thiave.

30. One to the people of Constantinopolis.

31. To Donatus of Mutugenna.[100]

32. To Cresconius, a grammarian.

33. An admonition to Festus in answer to the aforementioned.[101]

34. A letter to Maximinus, their bishop.

35. To the clerics who were converted from the party of Donatus.[102]

---

89. See ibid. II,39.
90. See ibid. II,40.
91. See ibid. II,46.
92. Ibid. II,59 Augustine notes that there were two books, although he thought that one should have been sufficient.
93. Letter 88.
94. Letters 106, 108.
95. Letter 93. This seems to be identical with the entry at VI,9.
96. Only Letter 33 has survived.
97. Only Letter 87 has survived.
98. Only Letter 66 has survived.
99. Letters 34-35.
100. Letter 173.
101. Letter 89.
102. Possibly Letter 144, which is addressed to all those who converted to Catholicism

36.   A letter to the tribune Dulcitius in answer to the aforementioned.[103]

37.   One letter to Gaudentius, a bishop of the Donatists.

SERMONS IN ANSWER TO THE DONATISTS

38.   Three on tradition, persecutions and false baptism.

39.   Again, one in answer to the aforementioned on the good of the unity of the Church, concerning those who complain that they are being coerced to unity.[104]

40.   Again, on the two women who quarreled over an infant,[105] in answer to the aforementioned, given at Sinitum.

41.   On testimonies from the scriptures in answer to the aforementioned and against idols.[106]

42.   In answer to the aforementioned on the birthday of the martyr Saint Salvus.

43.   In answer to the aforementioned, that it is not men who baptize but Christ.

44.   A very short [sermon] on baptism in answer to the aforementioned.

[VII.] IN ANSWER TO THE PELAGIANS

1.   Two books for Marcellinus on the baptism of infants, and a letter to him on the punishment and remission of sins.[107]

2.   One book for Marcellinus on the spirit and the letter.[108]

3.   One book on nature and grace.[109]

4.   One book for Bishops Eutropius and Paul on the perfection of the righteousness of man.

5.   One book in answer to the acts of Pelagius.[110]

6.   Two books for Pinianus, Albina and Melania, in answer to Pelagius and Caelestius, on the grace of Christ and original sin.[111]

7.   One book in answer to the questions of the Pelagians.

---

from the town of Cirta, and not merely to the clerics.
103. Letter 204.
104. Sermon 360C.
105. See 1 K 3:16-27.
106. Sermon 360A.
107. See *Revisions* II,33,
108. See ibid. II,37.
109. See ibid. II,42.
110. See ibid. II,47.
111. See ibid. II,50.

8.   Two books for Valerius on marriage and desire.[112]
9.   Four books for Pope Boniface in answer to the aforementioned.[113]
10. Six books in answer to Julian.[114]

LETTERS

11. Two letters to Xystus, a priest of the City,[115] in answer to the aforementioned.[116]
12. One letter to Mercator in answer to the same.[117]

***

13. A sermon on the baptism of infants.
14. One book for Valentine, a monk, on grace and free choice.[118]
15. Again, one book for the aforementioned on grace and rebuke.[119]
16. Again, an unfinished work in response to a second reply of Julian.[120]

[VIII.] AGAINST THE ARIANS

1.   A question on the Trinity.[121]
2.   Again, another on him who has always been born.[122]
3.   Again, on the equality of the Son.[123]
4.   Again, another on that which is written: *Then the Son himself will be subject to the one who has subjected everything to him* (1 Cor 15:28).[124]
5.   Fifteen books on the Trinity.[125]
6.   One book for Pascentius in answer to the aforementioned Arians.[126]

---

112. See ibid. II,53.
113. See ibid. II,61.
114. See ibid. II,62.
115. I.e., Rome.
116. Letters 191 and 194.
117. Letter 193.
118. See *Revisions* II,66.
119. See ibid. II,67.
120. *Unfinished Work in Answer to Julian.*
121. *A Miscellany of Eighty-three Questions* 18.
122. Ibid. 37.
123. Ibid. 50.
124. Ibid. 69.
125. See *Revisions* II,15.
126. Letter 238.

LETTERS

7. Two to the same person in answer to different questions.[127]
8. Letters to Helpidius in answer to the aforementioned.[128]
9. One to Terentianus.
10. One to Maximus.[129]

VARIOUS SERMONS AGAINST THE AFOREMENTIONED, WHO CONTEND THAT THE SON IS UNEQUAL TO THE FATHER

11. From the Gospel of John: *The Son cannot do anything on his own except what he sees the Father doing* (Jn 5:19).[130]
12. From the same John: *For the Father loves the Son and shows him all things* (Jn 5:20).
13. Again, on the Trinity, on *In the beginning was the Word* (Jn 1:1).[131]

***

14. A debate with Maximinus, a bishop of the Arians.
15. Again, two books for the aforementioned.
16. An unfinished work on heresies for the deacon Quodvultdeus.

[IX.] AGAINST THE APOLLINARIANS

One question.[132]

[X/1.] AGAIN, VARIOUS BOOKS AND SERMONS AND LETTERS COMPOSED FOR THE BENEFIT OF ALL THOSE WHO DESIRE TO LEARN

1. One book on the happy life for Theodore.[133]

---

127. Letters 239 and 241.
128. Letter 242. A second letter is promised in section 5, depending on Augustine's leisure, but it was probably lost.
129. Letter 170.
130. Sermon 126.
131. Sermon 117.
132. *A Miscellany of Eighty-three Questions* 80.
133. See *Revisions* I,2.

2. Two books of soliloquies.[134]
3. One book on grammar.[135]
4. Six books on music.[136]
5. The principles of the other disciplines, five books—namely, on dialectic, on rhetoric, on geometry, on arithmetic, on philosophy.[137]
6. One book on the magnitude of the soul.[138]
7. One book on the Teacher.[139]
8. One book on faith and the creed.[140]
9. One book on the Christian combat.[141]
10. Two books on the Sermon on the Mount in the gospel.[142]
11. Some commentaries on the Epistle to the Romans, two books.[143]
12. A commentary on the entire Epistle to the Galatians, one book.[144]

[X/2.]

1. A question as to why humankind is evil.[145]
2. Again, another as to whether an irrational animal can be happy.[146]
3. Again, another as to what the soul should properly be called in an ensouled being.[147]
4. Again, another as to whether the soul is moved by itself.[148]
5. Again, another on purifying the mind in order to see God.[149]
6. Again, another concerning by what evidence it is clear that human beings are superior to beasts.[150]
7. Again, another on the intellect.[151]

---

134. See ibid. I,4.
135. See ibid. I,6.
136. See ibid. I,11.
137. See ibid. I,6.
138. See ibid. I,8.
139. See ibid. I,12.
140. See ibid. I,17.
141. See ibid. II,3.
142. See ibid. I,19.
143. See ibid. I,23;25.
144. See ibid. I,24.
145. *A Miscellany of Eighty-three Questions* 4.
146. Ibid. 5.
147. Ibid. 7.
148. Ibid. 8.
149. Ibid. 12.
150. Ibid. 13.
151. Ibid. 15.

8.   Again, another on God's knowledge.[152]
9.   Again, another on God's place.[153]
10. Again, another on the difference of sins.[154]
11. Again, another as to whether everything has been created for the use of man.[155]
12. Again, another on how the soul's virtues were differentiated and defined by Cicero.[156]
13. Again, another on fear.[157]
14. Again, another as to whether nothing else should be loved than to lack fear.[158]
15. Again, another on what should be loved.[159]
16. Again, another on fostering charity.[160]
17. Again, another on the conformation of the soul.[161]
18. Again, another on foods.[162]
19. Again, another as to why, since God made all things, he did not make them in equal fashion.[163]
20. Again, another as to whether we may ever be able to see our thoughts.[164]
21. Again, another on what is written: *But it is good for me to cling to God* (Ps 73:28).[165]
22. Again, another on the hundred and fifty-three fish.[166]
23. Again, another on John the Baptist.[167]
24. Again, another on the ten virgins.[168]
25. Again, another: *But of the day and the hour no one knows, neither the angels of heaven nor the Son of Man but only the Father* (Mt 24:36).[169]

152. Ibid. 17.
153. Ibid. 20.
154. Ibid. 26.
155. Ibid. 30.
156. Ibid. 31.
157. Ibid. 33.
158. Ibid. 34.
159. Ibid. 35.
160. Ibid. 36.
161. Ibid. 38.
162. Ibid. 39.
163. Ibid. 41.
164. Ibid. 47.
165. Ibid. 54.
166. See Jn 21:6-11. *A Miscellany of Eighty-three Questions* 57.
167. *A Miscellany of Eighty-three Questions* 58.
168. See Mt 25:1-13. *A Miscellany of Eighty-three Questions* 59.
169. *A Miscellany of Eighty-three Questions* 60.

26. Again, another on what is written in the gospel, that on the mountain the Lord fed the crowds with five loaves.[170]

27. Again, another on what is written in the gospel, that *Jesus baptized more than John, although it was not he himself who baptized but his disciples* (Jn 4:1-2).[171]

28. Again, another on the Word.[172]

29. Again, another on the Samaritan woman.[173]

30. Again, another on the resurrection of Lazarus.[174]

31. Again, another on what is written: *Are you unaware, brothers (for I speak to those who know the law), that a person is subject to the law as long as he lives?* (Rom 7:1) up until the passage where it is written, *He will also give life to your mortal bodies through his Spirit dwelling within you* (Rom 8:11).[175]

32. Again, another on what is written: *For I think that the sufferings of this time are insignificant in comparison to the glory that is to come that will be revealed in us* (Rom 8:18), up until what is said: *For by hope we have been saved* (Rom 8:24).[176]

33. Again, another on what is written: *O man, who are you that you talk back to God?* (Rom 9:20)[177]

34. Again, another on what the Apostle says: *Death has been swallowed up in victory.*
Where, O death, is your struggle? Where, O death, is your sting. The sting of death is sin, but the strength of sin is the law. (1 Cor 15:54-56)[178]

35. Again, another on what is written: *Bear one another's burdens, and thus you will fulfill the law of Christ* (Gal 6:2).[179]

36. Again, another on the eternal times.[180]

37. Again, another on what is written in Paul's Epistle to the Colossians: *In whom we have redemption, the remission of sins, who is the image of the invisible God* (Col 1:14-15).[181]

---

170. See Jn 6:3-13. *A Miscellany of Eighty-three Questions* 61.
171. *A Miscellany of Eighty-three Questions* 62.
172. Ibid. 63.
173. See Jn 4:5-29. *A Miscellany of Eighty-three Questions* 64.
174. See Jn 11:17-44. *A Miscellany of Eighty-three Questions* 65.
175. *A Miscellany of Eighty-three Questions* 66.
176. Ibid. 67.
177. Ibid. 68.
178. Ibid. 70.
179. Ibid. 71.
180. Ibid. 72.
181. Ibid. 74.

38.   Again, another on God's inheritance.[182]
39.   Again, another on what the apostle James says: *Do you wish to know, O foolish person, that faith without works is useless?* (Jas 2:20).[183]
40.   Again, another on whether fear is a sin.[184]
41.   Again, another on the beauty of images.[185]
42.   Again, another on why Pharaoh's magicians performed certain miracles like Moses, the servant of God.[186]
43.   Again, another on Quadragesima and Quinquagesima.[187]
44.   Again, another on what is written: *Whom the Lord loves he corrects; he scourges every son whom he receives* (Heb 12:16).[188]
45.   Again, another on marriage.[189]

[X/3.]

1.   Four books on teaching Christianity.[190]
2.   Two books on different questions for Simplician.[191]
3.   A response to the objections of Hilary, one book.[192]
4.   Notes on the gospels, two books.[193]
5.   Notes on Job, one book.[194]
6.   Thirteen books of confessions.[195]
7.   One book of a catechism.[196]
8.   A response to the questions of Januarius, two books.[197]
9.   One book for Bishop Aurelius on the work of monks.[198]

---

182. Ibid. 75.
183. Ibid. 76.
184. Ibid. 77.
185. Ibid. 78.
186. See Ex 7-8. *A Miscellany of Eighty-three Questions* 79.
187. *A Miscellany of Eighty-three Questions* 81. Quadragesima was the forty-day period corresponding to present-day Lent. Quinquagesima was the fifty-day period between Easter and Pentecost.
188. Ibid. 82.
189. Ibid. 83.
190. See *Revisions* II,4.
191. See ibid. II,1.
192. See ibid. II,11.
193. See ibid. II,12.
194. See ibid. II,13.
195. See ibid. II,6.
196. See ibid. II,14.
197. See ibid. II,20.
198. See ibid. II,21.

10. An unfinished commentary on the Epistle of James, one book.[199]
11. Some commentaries on the Old Testament.[200]
12. One book on holy virginity.[201]
13. One book on the excellence of marriage.[202]
14. Twelve books on the literal meaning of Genesis.[203]
15. One [book] that the holy bishop Augustine began in his own hand for Quaternius.
16. Different questions on the Old Testament, in thirty-three books.[204]
17. One book in answer to Hilary on singing at the altar.[205]
18. One book for Honoratus on the grace of the New Testament.[206]
19. One book on faith and works.[207]
20. One book for Paulina on seeing God.[208]
21. One book on the perfection of man's justice.
22. One book for Saint Jerome on the origin of the soul.[209]
23. One book for the same person on a statement of the apostle James.
24. One book for Dardanus on the presence of God.[210]
25. For Casulanus on fasting on the sabbath.[211]
26. Four books for Victor on the nature of the soul and its origin.[212]
27. Two books for Pollentius on deficient marriages.[213]
28. Two books in answer to an adversary of the law and the prophets.[214]
29. One book against lying.[215]
30. One book for Laurence on faith, hope and charity.[216]

199. See ibid. II,32.
200. Very likely *Seven Books of Expressions in the Heptateuch* (see *Revisions* II,54) and *Seven Books of Questions on the Heptateuch* (see ibid. II,55).
201. See ibid. II,23.
202. See ibid. II,22.
203. See ibid. II,24.
204. This must surely be identical with the *Thirty-three Books in Answer to Faustus, a Manichean*, which is listed at IV,27 as *Different questions in response to Faustus, a Manichean, in thirty-three books.*
205. This is identical with *One Book in Answer to Hilary*, which is listed at X/3,3 as *A response to the objections of Hilary, in one book.*
206. See *Revisions* II,36.
207. See ibid. II,38.
208. See ibid. II,41.
209. This and the following book are Letters 166-167 and are treated as a single work in *Revisions* II,45.
210. See ibid. II,49.
211. Letter 36.
212. See *Revisions* II,56.
213. See ibid. II,57.
214. See ibid. II,58.
215. See ibid. II,60.
216. See ibid. II,63.

[X/4.]

1. Psalms commented on from the first to the thirty-second. Of these 18, 21, <25>, 26, 29, 30, 31 and 32 were preached to the people.[217]

2. Again, others dictated—namely 67, 71, 77, 78, 82, 87, 89, 104, 105, 107, 108, 110, 111, 112, 113, 114 and 115. Joined to these are 116, 117, 135 and 150.

3. All the rest, with the exception of 118, were preached to the people; they number ninety-seven.

4. All the sermons on the Psalms that were preached to the people, therefore, add up to one hundred twenty-three, because 121 is commented on twice.

5. [Again,] homilies on the Gospel of John from the beginning to the end, in six codexes.

[X/5.] LETTERS

Ten to Nebridius.[218]
To Hermogenianus.[219]
To Zenobius.[220]
To Firminus.
5. To Caelestinus.[221]
To Antoninus.
To Saturninus.
To Talasius and Valentinus.
To Eumatius.
10. To Gaius.[222]
To Licentius.[223]
To Desiderius.
To Bishop Valerius.[224]

---

217. Entries 1-4 here refer to what is known as a single work, the *Expositions of the Psalms*.
218. Letters 3, 4, 7, 9, 10, 11, 12, 13 and 14 have survived.
219. Letter 1.
220. Letter 2.
221. Letter 18.
222. Letter 19.
223. Letter 26.
224. Letters 21-22.

To Donatus.[225]
15. To Laetus.[226]
To Crato and other Carthaginians.
To Bishop Maximus.
To Profuturus.[227]
To Praesidius.
20. To Victor, a presbyter of Campus Bullensis.
To Anastasius.
To the monk Sebastian.
To Consentius.
To Bishop Boniface.[228]
25. To Romanianus.[229]
Again, to him.
To Bishop Paul.[230]
To his own people.[231]
Again, to them.
30. To Bishop Aurelius.[232]
Again, to him.[233]
Again, to him.[234]
To Bishop Alypius.[235]
Again, to him.
35. [Again, to him.]
To the presbyter Deogratias.[236]
Six to Jerome.[237]

---

225. Letters 100 and 173.
226. Letter 243.
227. Letter 38.
228. Letter 98.
229. Letter 15.
230. Letter 85.
231. Although Possidius lists nine letters, in various places among the catalogue of letters, as addressed to the faithful and/or clergy of Hippo, only three have survived: Letters 78, 122 and 268.
232. Letter 41.
233. Letter 60.
234. Letter 174 (prologue to *The Trinity*).
235. Possidius lists five letters to Alypius, but six have survived: Letters 29, 83, 125, 227, 9* and 10*.
236. Three letters to Deogratias have survived: 102 (*Six Questions Explained in Answer to the Pagans*), 173A and 25*.
237. Letters 28, 40, 67, 71, 73 and 82.

Eight to Paulinus.[238]
To Severinus.[239]

40. To Generosus.[240]
To Armentarius and Paulina.[241]
To Jovinus and Jovinianus and others.
Three to Bishop Evodius.[242]
To Proba on praying to God.[243]

45. Again, two to her.[244]
Again, to her and Juliana on the veiling of Demetrias.[245]
To Juliana on holy widowhood.[246]
Three to Honoratus.[247]
To Flaccianus.

50. Four to Nectarius.[248]
To Caecilianus.[249]
Two to Publicola.[250]
To Orontius.[251]
To Olimpius.[252]

55. To Cornelius.[253]
To Donatus.[254]
Again, to Olimpius.[255]
Two to his own people.
To the aforementioned Bishop Paul.

60. To Theodore.[256]

---

238. Letters 27, 31, 42, 45, 80, 95, 149 and 186.
239. Letter 52.
240. Letter 53.
241. Letter 127.
242. Letters 159, 162 and 164.
243. Letter 130.
244. On these only Letter 131 has survived.
245. Letter 150.
246. *The Excellence of Widowhood.*
247. Three letters are addressed to two different people of this name: Letter 49 to a Donatist bishop, and Letters 228 and 26* to a Catholic bishop.
248. Only Letters 91 and 104 have survived.
249. Letter 86.
250. Only one, Letter 47, has survived.
251. Letter 257.
252. Letter 96.
253. Letter 259.
254. Letter 100.
255. Letter 97.
256. Letter 61.

To Cresimus.[257]
To Victorinus.[258]
To Celer.[259]
To Caecilianus.

65. To Bishop Severus.[260]
To Bishop Novatus.[261]
To Felix.[262]
To Adeodatus.
[Again, to Bishop Novatus.][263]

70. To Catulinus.
To Faustus and Pelagia.
To Bishop Aurelius.[264]
To Eusebius.[265]
To Bishop Placentinus.

75. To Seleuciana.[266]
To Severus.[267]
To Bishop Memorius.[268]
To Asellus.
To Emilius.

80. To Theodore and Felicissimus.
To Apronianus and Avita.
To Florentina.[269]
To Mariniana.
To Bishop Innocent.[270]

85. To the emperors.
To Stilico.
To the prefects.

---

257. Letter 244.
258. Letter 59.
259. Letter 56.
260. Letter 62.
261. Letter 84.
262. Letter 252.
263. Letter 28*.
264. Letter 16*.
265. Two letters to Eusebius have survived: Letters 34-35.
266. Letter 265.
267. Letter 62.
268. Letter 101.
269. Letter 266.
270. Letter 175.

To Italica.[271]
To Crescens.
90.   To Bishop Olimpius.
To the deacon Restitutus.[272]
To Bishop Restitutus.
To Macharius.
To Domnio.
95.   To the presbyter Viventius.
To Delfinus.
Again, to Bishop Innocent.[273]
To Pammachius.
To Agrippinus.
100. To the people of Cataqua.
Again, to Bishop Aurelius.[274]
To Gerontius.
To Maximian.
Again, to Bishop Severus.[275]
105. To Felix and Hilarinus.[276]
Again, to his own people.
Again, to them.
Again, to them.
Again, to Bishop Innocent.[277]
110. To Maximus.[278]
To Burnius.
To his own priests.
Again, to Macharius.
To Theodulus.
115. To Concordius.
Again, to Bishop Memorius.
Again, to Crato.
Again, to Bishop Severus.[279]

271. Letter 92.
272. Letter 249.
273. Letter 176.
274. Letter 16*.
275. Letter 63.
276. Letter 77.
277. Letter 177.
278. Letter 17.
279. Letter 110.

To Novatus.
120. To the deacon Mercurius.
     To Romanus.
     Again, to the presbyter Emilius.
     Two to Theodore and Felicissimus.
     To Arator.
125. Again, two to Bishop Aurelius.
     To Firmus.[280]
     To Munerius.
     To Repentinus.
     To Pegasius and Vagulus.
130. To Bishop Ampelius.
     Again, to Repentinus.
     To Lauricius.
     To Maximus.[281]
     To Samsucius.
135. To Protogenus and Thalasius.
     Again, to Protogenus.
     Again, to Thalasius.
     Again, two to Protogenus.
     To Bishop Possidius.[282]
140. Again, to Bishop Aurelius.
     To the clergy of Carthage.
     To the monk Sebastian.
     To Cristinus.[283]
     To Anisius.
145. To Felix.[284]
     To Geminianus.
     Again, to the aforementioned Firmus.[285]
     To the grammarian Audax.[286]
     To Acacius.
150. To Cresconius.[287]

280. Letter 1A*.
281. Letter 170.
282. Letter 245.
283. Letter 256.
284. Letter 3*.
285. Letter 2*.
286. Letter 261.
287. Letter 113.

Again, to Bishop Alypius.
To Albina.[288]
To the proconsul Apringius.[289]
Again, to Cristinus.
155.	To Albina, Pinianus and Melania.[290]
To Romulus.[291]
To Pancarius.[292]
To Florentinus.[293]
To Cresconius.
160.	To Bishop Fortunatus.[294]
Again, to Generosus.[295]
Two to Bishop Benenatus.[296]
To Rusticus.[297]
To the presbyter Quintilianus.[298]
165.	To Xanctippus.[299]
Again, to Bishop Aurelius.
Again, to Celer.[300]
To Castorius.
Again, to Bishop Alypius.
170.	Again, two to Bishop Severus.
To Italica.[301]
To Lampadius.
To Fabiola.[302]
To Naucellio.[303]
175.	To the brothers at Carthage.
To Redemptus.

288. Letter 126.
289. Letter 134.
290. Letter 124.
291. Letter 247.
292. Letter 251.
293. Letter 114.
294. Letter 115.
295. Letter 116.
296. Letters 253-254.
297. Letter 255.
298. Letter 212.
299. Letter 65.
300. Letter 57.
301. Letter 99.
302. Letter 267.
303. Letter 70.

To the brothers at Carthage.
Again, to his own people.
To Maxima.[304]
180. One letter to Ecdicia.[305]
One letter to Peter and Abraham.[306]

[X/6.] VARIOUS SERMONS

1. On charity.[307]
2. On chaste fear.
3. On hope.
4. On what is written, *My yoke is easy and my burden is light* (Mt 11:30).[308]
5. On pleasing and on not pleasing men.
6. On what is written, *He will convict the world of sin, of justice and of judgment* (Jn 16:8).[309]
7. A sermon on part of Psalm 34.[310]
8. On the generations according to Matthew.
9. On Jacob and Esau.[311]
10. On the two blind men.[312]
11. On the son of Abraham led to sacrifice.[313]
12. Again, two on Abraham and his son.
13. On the three rods of Jacob[314] and on part of Psalm 21.[315]
14. On the ten strings.[316]
15. On the advantage of doing penance.
16. On Goliath and David[317] and on contempt for the world.[318]

---

304. Letter 264.
305. Letter 262.
306. 184/A.
307. Sermons 349-350A.
308. Sermons 69-70A.
309. Sermon 144.
310. *Exposition 1* or *2 of Psalm 34*.
311. See Gn 27:1-40. Sermon 4.
312. Sermon 88.
313. See Gn 22:1-19. Sermon 2.
314. See Gn 30:37-42.
315. See Ps 144:9. Sermon 4A.
316. Sermon 9.
317. See 1 S 17:1-58.
318. Sermon 32.

17. On the pilgrimage of Christians in this life.[319]

18. On the hundred and fifty-three fish from the Gospel of John.[320]

19. On Solomon's judgment between the two prostitutes.[321]

20. Two to young people on the day of the octaves of infants.[322]

21. On the verse of the Psalm, *God, I will sing to you a new song* (Ps 144:9).[323]

22. On the canticle of Isaiah.

23. On the canticle of Exodus.[324]

24. On Psalm 17 and the epistle of the apostle John.

25. On Psalm 21 and the epistle of blessed Peter the apostle.

26. On the responsory of the psalm, *Give us help from tribulation, and vain is salvation from man* (Ps 60:11).[325]

27. A sermon in which many questions are posed, but one is resolved.

28. Another in which questions posed from the Acts of the Apostles and from the gospel are resolved.[326]

29. On the calling of the apostle Paul and on the giving over of the Lord's Prayer.[327]

30. On Peter faltering on the sea.[328]

31. On part of Psalm 46.

32. On the burial of Bishop Cyrus of Carthage.

33. On the last day.[329]

34. On part of Psalm 71.

35. On part of Psalm 81.

36. On the birthday of Saint John.[330]

37. On the voice and the Word.[331]

38. On the Apostle, *For the end of the law is Christ* (Rom 10:4), and on a verse of Psalm 90, and on the gospel, *If the Son frees you, you will be truly free* (Jn 8:36).

---

319. Sermons 346, 346A and 346B.
320. See Jn 21:11. Sermons 248-252A.
321. See 1 K 3:16-28. Sermon 10.
322. Sermon 376A.
323. Sermon 33.
324. See Ex 15:1-21. Sermon 363.
325. Sermon 20B.
326. Sermon 149.
327. Sermon 278.
328. See Mt 14:24-33. Sermons 75-76.
329. Sermon 114B.
330. Sermons 287, 289-293D, 379-380.
331. Sermon 288.

39. On those who hunt for God and for the world.
40. On a verse of Psalm 103, and on the woman who was burdened with an infirmity and bent over for eighteen years.[332]
41. On what it says in Ecclesiasticus, *Every creature loves what is like itself, and all flesh sticks to what is like itself, and, if a wolf has sometimes been united with a lamb, so it is between the sinner and the righteous* (Sir 13:15-17).
42. On the Apostle, where it says, *For him who believes in him who justifies the wicked* (Rom 4:5), and, *The law is spiritual, but I am fleshly* (Rom 7:14), and so forth.
43. On a verse of Psalm 55 on the birthday of martyrs.
44. On a verse of Psalm 67, *As smoke dispersed, may they be dispersed* (Ps 68:2), and so forth.
45. From what the Apostle says, *According to the justice which is from the law he was without reproach* (Phil 3:6), and on a verse from Psalm 142.[333]
46. On a verse of Psalm 24, *Show me your ways, Lord* (Ps 25:4), and so forth.
47. On a verse of Psalm 41, *As the stag longs for streams of water* (Ps 42:1), and so forth.
48. On a verse of Psalm 109, where it says, *With you is the rule on the day of your strength* (Ps 110:3), and on Melchizedek.[334]
49. On the Apostle, *Wretched man that I am, who will free me from the body of this death?* (Rom 7:24)
50. On the woman who suffered a flow of blood, and on Jeremiah, where it says, *He took a linen loincloth and hid it in a rock* (Jer 13:2-5).
51. On the Apostle, *For you have died, and your life is hidden with Christ* (Col 3:3).
52. On the burial of Bishop Restitutus of Carthage.
53. On the gospel, *See, I am sending you like sheep in the midst of wolves* (Mt 10:16), and so forth.[335]
54. On obedience.[336]
55. On the advantage of fasting.[337]

---

332. See Lk 13:10-17.
333. Sermon 170.
334. See Gn 14:18-20.
335. Sermon 64.
336. Sermon 359B.
337. Sermon 400.

56. Again, on the advantage of doing penance, and on a verse of Psalm 50, *Have mercy on me, God* (Ps 51:1).

57. On the five porticos, where a great number of people were lying sick,[338] and on the Pool of Siloam.[339]

58. From what is written in Genesis, that God made the third day.[340]

59. Again, another on the fourth day.[341]

60. Another on the fifth day.[342]

61. Another on the sixth day.[343]

62. Another on the seventh day.[344]

63. On the drunkenness of Noah and on the nakedness of his thighs.[345]

64. On Jacob's wrestling with the angel.[346]

65. On the rod that was changed into a serpent,[347] and on the hand that turned color, and on the water that was changed into blood.[348]

66. From what Isaiah says, *But those who have been given to me shall possess the earth and shall inherit my holy mountain* (Is 57:13), and on the Apostle, *Beloved, having these promises, then* (2 Cor 7:1), and so forth.[349]

67. From the gospel on the shepherd, the hireling and the thief.[350]

68. On the Apostle, *No one ever hates his own flesh* (Eph 5:29), and from the gospel, *He who loves his soul will lose it* (Mt 10:39).

69. From what the Apostle says, *We brought nothing into this world* (1 Tm 6:7), and on a verse of Psalm 50, *Have mercy on me, God* (Ps 51:1), and from the gospel, *Do penance* (Mt 3:2).

70. From [a Book of] Kingdoms, on David's coming upon Bathsheba and seeing to it that her husband was slain.[351]

71. On a verse of Psalm 33, *Come, children, and hear me; I will teach you the fear of the Lord* (Ps 34:11), and on the woman caught in adultery who was brought to the Lord.[352]

---

338. See Jn 5:2-9.
339. See Jn 9:7. Sermon 125.
340. See Gn 1:9-13. Sermon 229S.
341. See Gn 1:14-19. Sermon 229T.
342. See Gn 1:20-23. Sermon 229U.
343. See Gn 1:24-31. Sermon 229V.
344. See Gn 2:1-3.
345. See Gn 9:21-24.
346. See Gn 32:26-33. Sermon 5.
347. See Ex 7:8-12.
348. See Ex 7:19-25.
349. Sermon 45.
350. See Jn 10:1-16. Sermon 137.
351. See 2 S 11:2-27.
352. See Jn 8:1-11.

72. From the gospel, *I am the way and the truth and the life* (Jn 14:6).[353]
73. A sermon given at Boset when the pagans came in.[354]
74. On the Apostle, *O, the depth [of the riches] of the wisdom and knowledge of God* (Rom 11:33), [and so forth], and on a verse of Psalm 59, *God, you rejected us and destroyed us* (Ps 60:1), and on a verse of Psalm 118, *It was good for me that you humbled me so that I would learn your righteous ways* (Ps 119:71).[355]
75. On a verse of Psalm 30, *In you, Lord, I have hoped; let me not be put to shame forever* (Ps 31:1).
76. On the works of mercy.
77. From the Gospel of John, where he inveighs against the ruler.
78. On unceasing charity.
79. On the responsory of Psalm 131, *I have prepared a lamp for my Christ* (Ps 132:17), and so forth.
80. On the responsory of Psalm 51, *I have hoped in God's mercy* (Ps 52:8).
81. On the responsory of Psalm 103, *Bless the Lord, my soul; Lord, my God, you are greatly magnified* (Ps 104:1).
82. On a reading from the Proverbs of Solomon, from the passage where it is said, *Who will find a valiant woman* (Prv 31:10), until the end of the book, namely, *And may her husband be praised in the gates* (Prv 31:31).[356]
83. From what is written in the Proverbs of Solomon, *There are those who pretend to be rich although they have nothing, and there are those who humble themselves although they are rich* (Prv 13:7), and, *The redemption of a man's soul is his riches, but a poor man does not endure threats* (Prv 13:8).[357]
84. On what is written in the Proverbs of Solomon, *Son, if you are wise, you will be wise for yourself and your neighbors, but if you turn out evil, you alone will suffer the evils* (Prv 9:12).[358]
85. On what is written in the gospel, *If your brother sins against you, correct him between yourself and him* (Mt 18:15), and in Solomon, *Gazing deceitfully with the eyes heaps up sadness for men, but he who reproves openly brings about peace* (Prv 10:10).[359]

353. Sermons 141-142.
354. Sermon 360B.
355. Sermon 159B.
356. Sermon 37.
357. Sermon 36.
358. Sermon 35.
359. Sermon 82.

86. On the gospel, where the Lord questions the Jews as to whose son they said the Christ was,[360] and on that widow who put two small coins in the almsbox.[361]

87. From the Gospel of Matthew, on the treasure in the field and the precious pearl and the net thrown into the sea.[362]

88. From the gospel, where the Lord does not want to be touched by Mary because he had not yet ascended to the Father.[363]

89. From the gospel, where the Lord commends his sheep to Peter.[364]

90. On the responsory of Psalm 56, *Have mercy on me, God, have mercy on me, for in you my soul confides* (Ps 57:1).

91. From the gospel, where it is written about the rich man who was clothed in purple and fine linen[365]

92. Two on the fortieth [day] of the Lord's ascension.[366]

93. On the fiftieth [day] during vigils, from what is written, *In the beginning God made heaven and earth* (Gn 1:1).[367]

94. Again, another on the same day, on the responsory of Psalm 140, *Lord, place a guard at my mouth* (Ps 141:3).

95. On the eight statements of the beatitudes from the gospel.[368]

96. Again, on the day of Pentecost, from what is written in Tobit, *On the day of Pentecost, which is holy for seven weeks* (Tb 2:1).

97. On the gospel, where it is written, *Come to terms with your opponent, when you are with him on the way* (Mt 5:25).

98. From the Apostle, on taking off the old man and putting on the new,[369] and on a verse of Psalm 25.

99. From the gospel, *I shall see you again, and your heart will rejoice* (Jn 16:22), and so forth.

100. On the birthday of the Lord.[370]

101. On the fortieth day of the Lord's ascension.[371]

---

360. See Mt 22:41-46.
361. See Mk 12:41-44 par.
362. See Mt 13:44-50.
363. See Jn 20:17.
364. See Jn 21:15-17.
365. See Lk 16:19-31. Sermons 113A-B, 367.
366. Sermons 261-265E, 377, 395.
367. See also entry 164.
368. See Mt 5:3-12. Sermon 53A.
369. See Col 3:9-10.
370. Sermons 184-196, 369-372.
371. See note 366.

102. From the gospel that is said, *The harvest* [*indeed*] *is great* (Mt 9:37), up until what is said, *Your peace will return to you* (Mt 10:13).

103. From the gospel on storing one's treasure in heaven.[372]

104. From the gospel where Jesus says to his disciples, *Until now you have asked for nothing in my name* (Jn 16:24).

105. On the birthday of the martyrs Castus and Emilius.[373]

106. [On the day of Pentecost.]

107. Again, on the day of Pentecost, on a verse of Psalm 140, *A just man will correct me in mercy* (Ps 141:5), [during vigils].[374]

108. Again, on the same day, on a verse of Psalm 117, *Confess to the Lord, for he is good* (Ps 118:1).

109. On the flame in the bush, and that it was not burned up,[375] for the fast during Quinquagesima.[376]

110. On a verse of Psalm 104, *Let the heart of those who seek the Lord rejoice* (Ps 105:3), again, during the fast of Quinquagesima.

111. On a verse of Psalm 115, *I said in my distress, Every man is a liar* (Ps 116:11).[377]

112. From the gospel, where Jesus said that he was not going up for the feast day, and yet he went up.[378]

113. From the Epistle to the Galatians, where Paul rebuked Peter.[379]

114. From the gospel, where Jesus caused a tree to wither up,[380] and on [the passage] where he pretended that he would continue on his way.[381]

115. On avarice.

116. On the Apostle, where he says, *He who boasts should boast in the Lord* (1 Cor 1:31), and on a verse of Psalm 70, *In your justice save me and deliver me* (Ps 71:2).[382]

117. On the gospel, where Martha served the Lord.[383]

118. On the birthday of [Saint] John the Baptist.[384]

---

372. See Mt 6:20 par.
373. Sermon 285.
374. Sermon 266.
375. See Ex 3:2.
376. Sermon 7.
377. Sermon 28A.
378. See Jn 7:2-10. Sermon 133.
379. See Gal 2:11-14. Sermon 162C.
380. See Mt 21:18-22.
381. See Lk 24:28. Sermon 89.
382. Sermon 160.
383. Lk 10:38-42. Sermons 103-104.
384. See note 330.

119. On the birthday of the apostles [Saints] Peter and Paul.[385]
120. From the gospel, on the love of God and neighbor.[386]
121. From the gospel, where the Pharisees ask the Lord if it is lawful to dismiss one's wife for any cause whatever.[387]
122. On the Apostle, where he says, *Who will separate us from the love of Christ?* (Rom 8:35)
123. From the gospel, *He who does not hate father and mother* (Lk 14:26-27), and so forth.
124. For the birthday of [Saint] Catulinus.
125. Two sermons for the birthday of the holy Scillitan martyrs.[388]
126. From the gospel, where Jesus says, *The times are fulfilled and the kingdom of God has drawn near; repent and believe in the gospel* (Mk 1:15).[389]
127. From the gospel, *Either make the tree good and its fruit good or make the tree bad and its fruit bad* (Mt 12:33).[390]
128. For the birthday of the martyr Saint Laurence.[391]
129. From the gospel, on the woman who was bent over for eighteen years,[392] and on those on whom a tower fell.[393]
130. For the birthday of the martyrs of the White Mass.[394]
131. For the birthday of the martyr Quadratus.[395]
132. From the gospel, *I am the bread that has come down from heaven* (Jn 6:41), and, *Work for the food that does not perish but that abides forever* (Jn 6:27).
133. On a verse of Psalm 17, *Your discipline has directed me to my end, and your discipline will teach me* (Ps 18:35).[396]
134. On a verse of Psalm 19, *May he send you help from the holy place* (Ps 20:2).

---

385. Sermons 295-299C, 381.
386. Sermon 90A.
387. See Mt 19:3-9.
388. Sermons 299D-F.
389. Sermon 94A.
390. Sermon 72.
391. Sermons 302-305A.
392. See Lk 13:10-17.
393. See Lk 13:4. Sermon 110A.
394. "White Mass": *Massa candida.* The term refers either to a large number of martyrs, who were covered with (white) lime during the persecution of Valerian, or to a place, otherwise unknown. Sermons 306-306A, 330.
395. Sermons 306C-D.
396. Sermon 14A.

135. On the gospel, where it says, *Do not fear those who kill the body* (Mt 10:28), and so forth.[397]
136. From the gospel, on the beatitudes.[398]
137. On the birthday of Saint Vincent.[399]
138. On a verse of Psalm 43, *For on your account we are being put to death* (Ps 44:22), and so forth.
139. For the birthday of Saint Agileius.
140. On the gospel, *Come to me, all who labor and are burdened, and I will give you rest* (Mt 11:28).[400]
141. Again, on the same reading, for the birth of the Carterii, on the love of God.
142. On the gospel reading, where Peter walked on the water at the Lord's command.[401]
143. On the day's ordination and the burial of Bishop Florentius.[402]
144. On electing and ordaining a bishop to replace the aforesaid.
145. On a verse of Psalm 7, *My just help is from the Lord, who saves those who are upright of heart* (Ps 7:10).
146. On a verse of Psalm 73, *Rise up, Lord, judge my cause; be mindful of the reproach of your servants* (Ps 74:22).
147. On a verse of Psalm 100, *To you, Lord, I shall sing of mercy and judgment* (Ps 101:1).
148. Ten sermons on the Epistle of the apostle John to the Parthians.
149. On a verse of Psalm 82, *God, who is like you? God, do not be silent and do not restrain yourself.* (Ps 83:1)[403]
150. On the birthday of Saint John the Baptist.[404]
151. On the ten plagues[405] and the ten commandments.[406]
152. On the gospel reading on the day of the martyrs.
153. From the Gospel of Luke and the Acts of the Apostles.
154. On a verse of Psalm 143, *God, I shall sing a new song to you* [*; I shall play for you on the ten-stringed psaltery*] (Ps 144:9).[407]

---

397. Sermon 65.
398. See Mt 5:3-12.
399. Sermons 274-277A.
400. See note 307.
401. See Mt 14:24-33. See note 328.
402. Sermon 396.
403. Sermon 24.
404. See note 329.
405. See Ex 7:14-12:34.
406. See Ex 20:1-17. Sermon 8.
407. Sermon 33.

155. On a reading from Isaiah, *Lord, who has believed what we have heard?* (Is 53:1)

156. From the gospel, *The one who loves his soul will lose it* (Jn 12:25), and so forth.[408]

157. Two sermons on the birthday of Saint John.[409]

158. On the birthday of the apostles Peter and Paul.[410]

159. From the gospel, *The Son cannot do anything on his own except what he sees the Father doing* (Jn 5:19).[411]

160. From the gospel, where the centurion pleads with the Lord on behalf of his son.[412]

161. On the wantonness of young people.[413]

162. On the three dead persons raised by the Lord.[414]

163. On what is written, *What eye has not seen* (1 Cor 2:9), and so forth.

164. On the day of Pentecost during vigils, on what is written, *In the beginning God made heaven and earth* (Gn 1:1).[415]

165. Two sermons on charity.[416]

166. On a verse of Psalm 70, *Free me from the hand of the sinner* (Ps 71:4), and so forth.[417]

167. On a verse of Psalm 74, *We shall praise you, God* (Ps 75:1), and so forth.[418]

168. On a verse of Psalm 117, *Praise the Lord, for he is good* (Ps 118:1).[419]

169. On the unity that has been preserved, for Maximus the primate.

170. Seven sermons on the birthday of the Lord.[420]

171. Seven sermons on the Epiphany.[421]

172. Five sermons on Quadragesima before Easter.[422]

---

408. Sermon 368.
409. See note 330.
410. See note 385.
411. Sermon 126.
412. See Mt 8:5-13 par. Sermons 62-62A.
413. Sermon 391.
414. See Mt 9:18-26 par.; Lk 7:11-15; Jn 11:1-44.
415. See also entry 93.
416. See note 307.
417. Sermon 22A.
418. Sermon 23A.
419. Sermons 29-29A.
420. See note 370.
421. Sermons 199-204A, 373-375.
422. Sermons 205-211A.

173. Two sermons on the passion of the Lord.[423]
174. Twenty-three sermons for the vigils of Easter.[424]
175. Three sermons on the Creed.[425]
176. One sermon on the Lord's Prayer.[426]
177. One exhortatory [sermon] to the *competentes*.[427]
178. Two sermons on the octaves of the *infantes*.[428]
179. Two sermons on the ascension of the Lord.[429]
180. Two sermons on the eucharist.
181. One sermon on the coming of the Holy Spirit.
182. One sermon on the birthday of the apostles.[430]
183. One sermon on the birthday of Saint John.[431]
184. Four sermons on the birthday of Saint Cyprian.[432]
185. Three sermons on the birthday of [Saints] Perpetua and Felicity.[433]
186. One sermon on the birthday of Saint Salvus.
187. Two sermons on the birthday of Saint Vincent.[434]
188. One sermon on the birthday of a bishop.
189. On a verse of Psalm 138, *Your eyes have seen my incompleteness* (Ps 139:16).
190. On the almsgiving of spiritual things.
191. On the ministry of fleshly things that is done toward the saints.
192. On the alms that are given to all.[435]
193. On Samson,[436] and on a verse of Psalm 57, *If, then, you truly speak justice [judge what is right]* (Ps 58:1).[437]
194. On the birthday of Saint Victor.

---

423. Sermons 218-218C.
424. Sermons 219-223K.
425. Sermons 212-215, 398.
426. Sermons 56-59
427. Sermon 216. The *competentes* were those who, at the beginning of Lent, had asked to be baptized at the Easter Vigil.
428. Sermons 260-260D, 353, 376. The *infantes* were those who had just been baptized at the Easter Vigil.
429. See note 354.Sermons 261-265F, 377, 395
430. These are probably the apostles Peter and Paul. See note 385.
431. See note 330.
432. Sermons 308A-313F.
433. Sermons 280-282, 394.
434. See note 398.
435. Sermon 164A.
436. See Jgs 13:24-16:31.
437. Sermon 364.

195. On a verse of Psalm 115, *Precious in the sight of the Lord is the death of his holy ones* (Ps 116:15).
196. On Susanna[438] and Joseph.[439]
197. On a verse of Psalm 131, *Let your priests be clothed in righteousness* (Ps 132:9).
198. Two sermons on the dedication of a church.[440]
199. On blasphemy against the Holy Spirit.[441]

***

200. On the care to be taken of the dead.[442]
201. One book for Dulcitius.[443]
202. One sermon on continence.

***

And so, for the instruction of souls, the aforementioned holy bishop Augustine, impelled by the Holy Spirit, in the holy Catholic Church, produced books, sermons and letters to the number of one thousand and thirty, apart from those that cannot be numbered because he himself did not give them a number.

Here ends the catalogue of all the books of the venerable bishop Augustine.

438. See Dn 13.
439. See Gn 39:6-18. Sermon 343.
440. Sermons 336-338.
441. Sermon 71.
442. See *Revisions* II,64.
443. See ibid. II,65.

Appendix II

Based on the table established by Goulven Madec in Nuova Biblioteca Agostiniana I/II, cxxii-cxxiv.

Revisions	Work	*Indiculus*
I,1	Three books in answer to the Academics	I,1
I,2	One book on the happy life	X,/1,1
I,3	Two books on order	I,2
I,4	Two books of soliloquies	X/1,2
I,5	One book on the immortality of the soul	I,3
I,6	[Books on the disciplines]	X/1,3-5
I,7	Two books on the Catholic way of life and the Manichean way of life	IV,1
I,8	One book on the magnitude of the soul	X/1,6
I,9	Three books on free choice	IV,3
I,10	Two books on Genesis against the Manicheans	IV,5
I,11	Six books on music	X/1,4
I,12	One book on the Teacher	X/1,7
I,13	One book on true religion	I,5
I,14	One book on the advantage of believing	I,4
I,15	One book on the two souls	IV,2
I,16	The acts of a debate with Fortunatus, a Manichean, in one book	IV,6
I,17	One book on faith and the creed	X/1,8
I,18	One book of an unfinished literal commentary on Genesis	——
I,19	Two books on the Lord's Sermon on the Mount	X/1,10
I,20	A psalm against the party of Donatus, in one book	VI,1
I,21	One book in answer to a letter of the heretic Donatus	VI,2
I,22	One book in answer to Adimantus, a disciple of Mani	IV,4
I,23	A commentary on some statements in the Apostle's Epistle to the Romans, in one book	X/1,11
I,24	A commentary on the Epistle to the Galatians, in one book	X/1,12

I,25	An unfinished commentary on the Epistle to the Romans, in one book	X/1,11
I,26	One book containing a miscellany of eighty-three questions	I,6-19; IX
I,27	One book on lying	——
II,1 (28)	Two books for Simplician	X/3,2
II,2 (29)	One book in answer to the letter of Mani know as *The Foundation*	IV,6
II,3 (30)	One book on the Christian combat	X/1,9
II,4 (31)	Four books on teaching Christianity	X/3,1
II,5 (32)	Two books against the party of Donatus	VI,3
II,6 (33)	Thirteen books of confessions	X/3,6
II,7 (34)	Thirty-three books in answer to Faustus, a Manichean	IV,27
II,8 (35)	Two books in answer to Felix, a Manichean	IV,25
II,9 (36)	One book on the nature of the good	IV,26
II,10 (37)	One book in answer to Secundinus,	IV,24
II,11 (38)	One book in answer to Hilary	X/3,17
II,12 (39)	Questions on the gospels, in two books	X/3,4
II,13 (40)	Notes on Job, in one book	X/3,5
II,14 (41)	One book on instructing beginners in the faith	X/3,7
II,15 (42)	Fifteen books on the Trinity	VIII,5
II,16 (43)	Four books on the agreement among the evangelists	I,20
II,17 (44)	Three books in answer to a letter of Parmenian	VI,4
II,18 (45)	Seven books on baptism	VI,5
II,19 (46)	One book in answer to what Centurius, one of the Donatists, presented	VI,12
II,20 (47)	Two books in answer to the questions of Januarius	X/3,8
II,21 (48)	One book on the work of monks	X/3,9
II,22 (49)	One book on the excellence of marriage	X/3,13
II,23 (50)	One book on holy virginity	X/3,12
II,24 (51)	Twelve books on the literal meaning of Genesis	X/3,14
II,25 (52)	Three books in answer to the writings of Petilian	VI,6-8
II,26 (53)	Four books in answer to Cresconius, a grammarian of the Donatist party	VI,11
II,27 (54)	One book of proofs and testimonies in answer to the Donatists	——
II,28 (55)	One book in answer to a certain Donatist	——
II,29 (56)	A notice to the Donatists about the Maximianists, in one book	——
II,30 (57)	One book on demonic divination	I,22
II,31 (58)	Six questions explained in answer to the pagans	I,21
II,32 (59)	A commentary on the Epistle of James to the twelve tribes	X/3,10

II,33 (60)	Three books for Marcellinus on the punishment and remission of sins and on the baptism of infants	VII,1
II,34 (61)	One book for Constantine on the one baptism in answer to Petilian	VI,13
II,35 (62)	One book on the Maximianists in answer to the Donatists	VI,14
II,36 (63)	One book for Honoratus on the grace of the New Testament	X/3,18
II,37 (64)	One book for Marcellinus on the spirit and the letter	VII,2
II,38 (65)	One book on faith and works	X/3,19
II,39 (66)	A summary of the conference with the Donatists, in three books	VI,15
II,40 (67)	One book in answer to the Donatists after the conference	VI,16
II,41 (68)	One book on seeing God	X/3,20
II,42 (69)	One book on nature and grace	VII,3
II,43 (70)	Twenty-two books on the city of God	I,23
II,44 (71)	One book for Orosius in refutation of the Priscillianists and the Origenists	V,1
II,45 (72)	Two books for the presbyter Jerome, one on the origin of the soul and another on a phrase of James	X/3,22-23
II,46 (73)	One book for Emeritus, a bishop of the Donatists, after the conference	VI,18
II,47 (74)	One book on the acts of Pelagius	VII,5
II,48 (75)	One book on the correction of the Donatists	VI,17
II,49 (76)	One book for Dardanus on the presence of God	X/3,24
II,50 (77)	Two books for Albina, Pinianus and Melania, in answer to Pelagius and Caelestius, on the grace of Christ and original sin	VII,6
II,51 (78)	The proceedings with Emeritus, a bishop of the Donatists, after the conference, in one book	——
II,52 (79)	One book in answer to a sermon of the Arians	——
II,53 (80)	Two books for Count Valerius on marriage and desire	VII,8
II,54 (81)	Seven books on expressions	——
II,55 (82)	Seven books of questions	——
II,56 (83)	Four books on the soul and its origin	X/3,26
II,57 (84)	Two books for Pollentius on adulterous marriages	X/3,27
II,58 (85)	Two books in answer to an adversary of the law and the prophets	X/3,28
II,59 (86)	Two books in answer to Gaudentius, a bishop of the Donatists	VI,19
II,60 (87)	One book against lying	X/3,29
II,61 (88)	Four books in answer to two letters of	VII,9

Index of Scripture

(prepared by Michael T. Dolan)

Index

(prepared by Kathleen Strattan)

The first numeral in the Index is the Book number.
The numbers following the commas are the Chapter, then the Section numbers.
(In Chapter I,26, in *A Miscellany of Eighty-Three Questions*,
these are also followed by Question numbers.)

211

corpses, I,26(25),2,51
corruption; corruptible things,
    I,22(21),3
creation, I,15(14),1; I,26(25),2,19
    See also world; *specific topics*
    and equality, I,26(25),2,41
    freed from slavery to destruction,
        I,26(25),2,67
    man and, I,26(25),2,30
    And thus it was done, II,54(81)
    twofold, I,13(12),2
Cresconius (Donatist grammarian),
    II,26(53)
crimes
    See also punishment
    and free choice, I,9(8),3
    and God's justice, I,9(8),3
cross, I,26(25),2,25
    See also thief
    *my God, why have you forsaken
        me,* II,36(63)
Cyprian, I,1,3; II,1(28),1; II,18(45);
    II,28(55)

Dardanus, Claudius Postumus,
    II,49(76)
darkness, II,36(63)
David, King, I,26(25),2,61;
    II,1(28),2; II,16(43)
death, I,19(18),5
    See also resurrection of the body
    care to be taken of the dead,
        II,64(91)
    corpses, I,26(25),2,51
    as from God, I,26(25),2,21
    God did not make death,
        I,26(25),2,21
    "God seeks the death of no one,"
        I,21(20),2
    grieving death of a friend,
        II,6(33),2
    life after, II,43(70),1
    necessity of dying,
        I,26(25),2,66

and procreation of children,
    II,22(49),1; II,53(80)
sin and, I,13(12),4; I,19(18),7;
    I,26(25),2,66;
    I,26(25),2,70
swallowed up in victory,
    I,23(22),1; I,26(25),2,70
"they will not sense death,"
    II,33(60)
Where, O death, is your strife?,
    I,19(18),2
deformity, II,62(89)
demons, I,13(12),6
    demonic divination, II,30(57)
Deogratias, II,31(58)
desire
    See also concupiscence; lust;
        sexual relations
    marriage and, II,53(80)
devil, I,15(14),7
    Book of Job, I,15(14),7
    and his angels, I,15(14),7; II,14(41)
dialectic, I,6
diet. *See* food
discipline: knowledge and, I,5,2
discipline (punishment). *See*
    punishment
disciplines, I,6
    See also liberal disciplines
Donatists, II,5(32); II,36(63)
    See also Conference of Carthage
    answer to "certain Donatist,"
        II,28(55)
    and baptism, II,18(45)
    Centurius, II,19(46)
    correction of, II,48(75)
    Cresconius, II,26(53)
    Donatus, answer to, I,21
    Emeritus, II,46(73); II,51(78)
    Gaudentius of Thamugadi,
        II,59(86)
    and Maximianists, II,29(56);
        II,35(62)
    *Notice to the Donatists about the
        Maximianists,* II,29(56)

hate
  No one ever hates his own flesh,
      I,26(25),2,36
  for parents and children
      (explanation of),
      I,19(18),5
  The pride of those who hate you,
      I,19(18),8
"hearers" (Manicheans), II,10(37)
heaven
  See also specific topics, e.g.,
      resurrection of the body
  Jesus in, I,26(25),2,42
  new heaven and the new earth,
      I,4,3
  returning "more safely" to, I,1,3
  today you will be with me in
      paradise, I,26(25),2,62
Hebrews, Epistle to, II,22(49),2
Hebrews (people), II,16(43)
Heli, II,7(34),2
hell, I,7(6),6
  See also punishment
Heptateuch:
  seven books of questions,
      II,55(82)
  seven books on expressions,
      II,54(81)
heresy; heretics, II,28(55)
  See also error; schism; *individual*
      names/groups, e.g.,
      Donatists; Jovinian
heretics, "recent." *See* Pelagians
high priests, II,55(82),2
Hilary, II,11(38)
Holy of Holies, II,55(82),2
Holy Spirit, I,23(22),2; I,24(23),2
  as dove, I,26(25),2,43
  gift of, I,23(22),1–3
  sin against, I,25(24)
honor, II,18(45)
Honoratus, I,14(13); II,36(63)
Honorius, Emperor, II,26(53);
      II,51(78)

hope:
  faith, charity and, II,63(90)
  happiness and, I,4,3
  by hope we have been saved,
      I,26(25),2,67
  soul and, I,4,3
human beings
  See also man; *specific topics,* e.g.,
      death
  as either foolish or wise,
      I,14(13),4
  superior to animals, I,26(25),2,13
human nature, I,13(12),8
human race, ages of, I,26(25),2,44
hymns, II,11(38)

ideas, I,26(25),2,46
ignorance: *I obtained mercy because*
      I acted in ignorance, I,9(8),5
image of God, I,18(17);
      I,26(25),2,51; I,26(25),2,67
  Adam and, II,24(51),2
  image of the invisible God,
      I,26(25),2,74
  the Son as, I,18(17)
images, beauty of, I,26(25),2,78
immortality, I,22(21),3
  See also under soul: immortality of
  of Christ, I,24(23),1
incense, II,55(82),2
incorruption, I,22(21),3
infants
  See also under baptism; original sin
  Pelagian beliefs regarding,
      I,15(14),2; I,15(14),6;
      II,33(60)
infinity, I,26(25),2,32
Innocent, bishop of Rome, II,50(77)
intellect, I,26(25),2,15
  See also knowledge; mind
intelligible world, I,3,2
invisible things, I,11(10),1
  image of the invisible God,
      I,26(25),2,74

serpents, I,10(9),2
*This serpent which you fashioned
to make a mockery of
him,* I,15(14),7
Sextus (philosopher), II,42(69)
sexual relations, II,22(49),1–2
See also concupiscence; desire; lust
becoming unclean through,
II,55(82),2
deformity and, II,62(89)
Increase and multiply, I,10(9),2
procreation of children,
II,22(49),1; II,53(80)
and sin, I,10(9),2; I,13(12),8
shamefulness, II,18(45)
sheep: with variegated young,
II,55(82),1
silver, I,26(25),2,53; II,18(45)
Simplician, II,1(28)
sin
See also evil; free choice;
original sin; punishment;
remission; wickedness
and death, I,26(25),2,66;
I,26(25),2,70
difference of sins, I,26(25),2,26
forgiveness/remission of,
I,25(24); I,26(25),2,74;
II,33(60)
and God's mercy, I,26(25),2,68
a good person and, I,15(14),2
grace and, I,25(24); I,26(25),2,66;
II,50(77)
and guilt, I,15(14),2; I,15(14),5–6
against the Holy Spirit, I,25(24)
involuntary, I,13(12),5
and the law, I,26(25),2,70
and loving bodily things,
I,15(14),7–8
nature and, I,1,2; I,15(14),7
as outside the body, II,15(42),3
and repentance, I,26(25),2,68
and separation from God, I,5,2
"sin harms no one's nature but
one's own," I,10(9),3

as voluntary evil, I,13(12),5
and will, I,9(8),3; I,13(12),5;
I,15(14),2–6; I,16(15),2;
I,19(18),3; I,26(25),2,24
sinners: God hearing, I,3,3
sin unto death, I,19(18),7
Sirach, Jesus, II,4(31),2
Sixtus, bishop of Rome, II,42(69)
skepticism. *See* Academics
slavery:
to destruction, I,26(25),2,67
slave as master's friend, I,8(7),4
sobriety, I,7(6),3
Sodom, II,1(28),1
Soliloquies, I,4; I,5,1
Solomon, II,19(46)
See also Wisdom of Solomon
re. the Son of God, II,31(58)
Son of God, I,26(25),2,16;
I,26(25),2,23
See also Jesus Christ
according to Solomon, II,31(58)
*But on the day and hour no one
knows,* I,26(25),2,60
equality of, I,26(25),2,50
and Father as one, I,4,3
as likeness of the Father, I,18(17)
as man, I,26(25),2,43
*subjected to the one who has
subjected everything to
him,* I,26(25),2,69
sons
See also Aaron, sons of
the term, I,22(21),3
Soranus of Ephesus, II,62(89)
soul; souls, I,26(25),2,1
See also spirit
Adam as *made into a living soul,*
I,10(9),3; I,13(12),4
in an ensouled being, I,26(25),2,7
angels and, I,11(10),4; I,16(15),2
binding our souls, I,13(12),9
and body, I,5,3
conformation of, I,26(25),2,38
happy life and, I,2; I,4,3